How *Not* to
Get Ripped Off

The HOW TO Series

HOW TO COPE WITH CREDIT AND DEAL WITH DEBT
Ann Andrews and Peter Houghton

HOW TO FACE THE INTERVIEW
And Other Selection Procedures
Clive Fletcher

HOW TO FORM A LIMITED COMPANY
Complete With All The Forms You Need
Barry Sheppard

HOW NOT TO GET RIPPED OFF
The Complete Consumer Guide
Barbara Lantin

HOW TO PASS EXAMS
And How To Prepare For Them With Less Anxiety
Fred Orr

HOW TO SPEAK IN PUBLIC
A Winning Way With Words
Dick Smithies

HOW TO SPLIT UP – AND SURVIVE FINANCIALLY
Tony Hetherington

HOW TO SUCCEED AT WORK
Fred Orr

How *Not* to Get Ripped Off

The Complete Consumer Guide

BARBARA LANTIN

London
UNWIN PAPERBACKS
Sydney   Boston   Wellington

First published by Unwin Paperbacks, 1987 an imprint of
Unwin Hyman Ltd.

UNWIN HYMAN LIMITED
Denmark House
37–39 Queen Elizabeth Street
LONDON SE1 2QB
and
40 Museum Street, London WC1A 1LU

Allen & Unwin Australia Pty Ltd
8 Napier Street, North Sydney, NSW 2060, Australia

Unwin Paperbacks with Port Nicholson Press
60 Cambridge Terrace, Wellington, New Zealand

British Library Cataloguing in Publication Data

Lantin, Barbara
　How not to get ripped off? the complete consumer guide.–
(The how to series)
1. Consumer education – Great Britain
I. Title　II. Series
640'.73'0941　TX335
ISBN 0–04–346004–6

Set in 10 on 11 point Palatino by Bedford Typesetters Ltd
and printed in Great Britain by Cox & Wyman Ltd, Reading

Contents

Acknowledgements

So many people have helped with the preparation of this book that it would be impossible to list them by name. I am indebted to all of them. I would particularly like to thank June Doyle at the Department of Trade and Industry for patiently answering my numerous enquiries; Gwyneth Davies for her invaluable tips and ideas; and Wendy Toms and Richard Thomas for their advice and encouragement over more years than I care to remember. I would also like to thank my husband Jeffrey for his patience during the writing of this book and his constructive criticisms at the end of it and my children Rachel, Daniel and Nicholas for the diversions they provided.

Introduction

Have you ever bought something and almost instantly regretted your decision – a new coat which looked pale grey in the shop but was actually a bilious shade of green in the daylight; or a washing machine so noisy you had to leave the kitchen while it was in operation? Have you ever picked a plumber out of the Yellow Pages with a pin and found out – too late – that you could have installed a new central heating system for what he charged to mend your leaking radiator valve? Have you ever booked a package tour hotel only to discover that the 'modestly furnished' bedrooms would have made a prison cell look palatial by comparison? In short, have you ever felt that you have spent your money unwisely – possibly through no fault of your own?

If you can honestly answer 'no' to that question, then you are either very canny or very lucky and probably don't need this book. But how many of us can make that claim? Official statistics show that every year hundreds of thousands of people complain to advice centres and local authority officers about goods and services with which they are dissatisfied; and it is acknowledged that hundreds of thousands more simply moan to friends and family, but take no positive action.

Some of these people are the prey of rogues, some the victims of incompetence or ignorance. Others have simply made a bad buy and have nobody to blame for their dissatisfaction but themselves. This book is aimed at all those groups. It has two roles: prevention and cure. Follow the 'buy-laws', which you'll find in most chapters, *before* you choose your washing machine, plumber or package tour and you should end up smiling rather than swearing. But if you *do* have cause to complain, the book explains how to present your case so that you have the best chance of success. And if complaining fails to solve the problem, the final chapter tells you how to take your case to court.

No book of this kind can be written without reference to the law. But this is not a legal textbook; it is a practical guide. Knowing your rights at law takes you only half way along the road to a fair deal. I hope that the advice contained in this book, which is distilled from my experiences over almost a decade of writing about consumer matters, will guide you the rest of the way.

The book deals mainly with the position in England and Wales, although most of the advice applies to the whole of the United Kingdom. Where the situation in Scotland and Northern Ireland differs significantly from that in the rest of the country, I have made this clear. However, it is impossible to list all the differences. If you are uncertain about the law in your part of the country, consult a Consumer Advice Centre, Citizens' Advice Bureau or a solicitor.

The organisations mentioned in this book are listed in alphabetical order at the end.

1

Going Shopping

Before You Buy

The first lesson in learning to be a clever consumer is to think before you buy. Mistakes are annoying, expensive – and usually avoidable. Wise buying may take time, though not as much as you might imagine, but it saves wasted money and wasted regrets in the long run.

Whenever you shop, but especially when you are making the kind of purchase that you expect to last you for some time, follow the 'buy-laws':

☞ Decide in advance how much you want to spend.

☞ Do your homework. Think carefully about exactly what you want and need (you will find some guidelines below) and *why* you are buying.

☞ Don't impulse buy.

☞ Don't let a persuasive shop assistant rush you into buying before you are ready.

☞ Don't be afraid to leave empty-handed.

☞ Shop around: prices vary enormously.

Doing your homework
Buying on the spur of the moment – at sale time for example – can land you a winner if you are lucky. But it is far more sensible to do your bargain hunting armed with a shopping list compiled after careful thought. That way, you are less likely to be dazzled by the prospect of all the money you could save into buying something you don't really want anyway. So what sort of research *can* you do beforehand?

* If you are replacing something you have had before – a washing machine, say, or a three-piece suite – make a list of the points you do and do not like about your present model.

If you are buying something for the first time – a micro-wave oven perhaps – start by browsing in shops with a wide selection. Ask a sales assistant to describe the main points of a few types to you and pick up any manufacturers' leaflets which are on display. If none are visible, ask. It is also worth asking your friends' opinions of the models they own.

* Think about the features which are important to you. With a washing machine, these might include the spin speed, whether there are any 'economy' buttons and how much noise it makes. With a three-piece suite you might want to know whether the covers are removable and washable and whether you are likely to be able to buy extra pieces in the future. Consider how your new purchase will fit into your home in terms of space, style and colour.

* Find out about maintenance and servicing, if this applies. If you are buying an electrical appliance and will want to do basic repairs yourself, how easy are these to perform? I once owned an extremely efficient vacuum cleaner which required 15 minutes and a special screwdriver to change the drive belt. If you are likely to need an engineer, try to find out about the service arrangements. Is there a service centre near you and are

spare parts easy to obtain? Friends with appliances made by the same manufacturer should be able to give an idea of how smoothly the system works.

* There are various types of symbols used these days to help you identify products which are safe and of high quality. I describe these in more detail in Chapter 4.

* Finally, think about the future. Are your needs likely to change during the lifetime of the item you are about to buy? If you want a freezer, for example, and plan to start a family within a few years, pick the largest you can afford that will fit into your home. If you need a new dining room carpet and think you might make this a playroom as the children grow up, choose one that is practical as well as pretty.

Getting help
Once you have decided what you want and need from your new purchase, there are various aids to help you pick the right model.

* *Which?* magazine, published by the Consumers' Association, carries out tests on a vast range of different products and highlights those it considers to be 'best buys', 'worth a look' and 'good value'. It is kept by many libraries.

* The Good Housekeeping Institute tests household appliances for *Good Housekeeping* magazine. If you write to them enclosing a stamped addressed envelope and describing in some detail what you want to buy, they will tell you which models have done well in their tests. For a fee they will also send you a copy of the test report.

* Consumer Advice Centres have trained staff who can give you useful information before you shop. They will help you work out what your needs are and advise you on what is available. But they will not recommend particular products or shops. CACs tend to be found in large cities. The trading standards or consumer pro-

tection department at your local council offices should be able to tell you whether there is a CAC in your area.

* When you have narrowed down your choice to just a few candidates, go to a shop which stocks them and ask a sales assistant who is not too busy to go over them with you. If he does not seem very interested or well informed, ask to see somebody more senior. Don't forget to ask about the drawbacks as well as the advantages. Remember that some staff in shops are actually representatives of a particular manufacturer: they invariably wear a badge indicating this. What you may not realise is that some manufacturers and retailers offer sales assistants rewards (called 'incentives' in the trade) for selling a particular line – because it is slow moving, perhaps. There is nothing wrong with this (as long as the shop manager knows what is going on) except that you may be persuaded to buy something which doesn't quite meet your needs because the shop assistant stands to gain by the sale. For this reason it is a good idea to seek advice in more than one shop.

Where to buy

Once you have made your shortlist, shop around for the best price. Compare department stores with discount warehouses and smaller specialist shops. If you want the item delivered, ask whether there is a charge. If you are paying by credit, work out what your purchase is going to cost in total. There is little point buying your new cooker at one shop for £270 and then spending £30 in interest charges so you can spread the payments over a year when the shop across the road is selling the same model at £285 with a year's interest-free credit thrown in.

Price may be the main consideration when choosing where to buy, but it is not the only one. The fact that you saved yourself £10 by buying your washing machine at Heretoday Stores will be scant consolation to you if the appliance packs up on you after three months and you return to the shop to find the premises are now occupied by an off-licence. Ask friends which shops in the area they have found obliging. Some local consumer groups keep a 'whitelist' of traders recommended by their members and are willing to pass this information on to non-members. The National Federation of Consumer Groups can tell you whether there is a group in your area.

Some retailers belong to trade associations which have drawn up codes of practice with the backing of the Office of Fair Trading. These codes cover things like the kind of information you should be given when you shop, the sort of service you should receive and how complaints should be handled. I look at them in more detail in Chapter 3. Although there is no doubt that codes of practice have improved standards of customer service in some sectors – in car and shoe retailing, for example – some shop assistants, sadly, still seem completely unaware of their existence. Shops which adhere to a code usually have a sticker to this effect on the door and entering one should – in theory at least – mean you get a reasonable standard of service.

Finally, when you have decided what you are going to buy and where, talk your decision over with a sales assistant at your chosen shop to make sure the product will meet your particular needs. This discussion could be important if you have problems later.

Prices

What is a bargain?
The scene is a high street. Two stores are selling identical stereo systems. One carries a sign saying 'Was £250. Now £220'. The other price tag simply reads '£209.99'. Which shop attracts the customers? Not the second with its lower price, but the first. For the offer of an apparent bargain, shining like a beacon, dazzles shoppers into buying with their eyes closed. This tale, said to be true, is an illustration of the power of a price reduction.

Everybody welcomes genuine bargains, but not all price reductions are what they seem. The law is meant to prevent you from being misled, but it is riddled with loopholes and often flagrantly ignored: completely new legislation looks likely soon. In the meantime, be warned that some traders will try almost anything to convince customers that they are saving money when they are not.

Minimum and maximum prices

There was a time when shopping around was a waste of energy because prices for many goods were much the same everywhere – fixed by the manufacturers and distributors before their products reached the shops. Today, resale price maintenance, as this price-fixing is called, is banned for virtually all goods and it is up to individual retailers to decide what to charge for their wares. However, the Restrictive Practices Court does have the power to approve resale price maintenance for certain categories of goods, and has done so for books and for non-prescription medicines. That is why you will find wide variations between different shops in the price of, say, a T-shirt or a toaster, but none in the price of a new paperback or a packet of aspirin. Manufacturers of other kinds of goods have been known to try to dictate the price at which their products are sold by refusing to supply shops which offer them at a discount. But this practice is also unlawful under the Resale Prices Act 1976.

Recommended prices

Although manufacturers must not *set* prices for their products, they are allowed to *recommend* prices. But it is up to the retailer to decide what he actually charges.

One way a shopkeeper can make it look as if he is offering a price reduction when he is not is to compare his price with the Manufacturer's Recommended Price, the Recommended Retail Price or Suggested Selling Price – sometimes called the MRP, RRP or SSP. The goods may never have been on sale in his shop or anywhere else at the Manufacturers'

Recommended Price, so the comparison may be totally meaningless.

Because of this, the government has banned comparisons with MRPs for certain types of goods. Under the Price Marking (Bargain Offers) Order 1979, retailers must not compare their prices with MRPs, RRPs or SSPs when they sell:

- most domestic electrical and gas appliances
- consumer electronic goods such as stereos, radios and televisions
- furniture
- beds, mattresses and headboards
- carpets
- portable space heaters.

But these phoney discounts have not been eliminated completely. Retailers selling other types of product can and often do quote MRPs that bear no relation to the price at which the goods are actually available in the shops: in one survey of 168 items carried out by the National Federation of Consumer Groups, only 11 were on sale at a price near or above the recommended retail price. Another ploy, sometimes used by furniture stores, is to 'discount' something sold in kit form from a so-called 'ready-assembled price' or RAP, when that item is never actually sold assembled by the trader.

Simon Simple saw a gold watch in the window of his local jewellers. The price ticket said 'Manufacturer's Recommended Price £75. Our price £60'. Thinking he was getting a bargain, Simon bought one. The following week he saw the same watch in a neighbouring town for £50. He complained to the shop where he had bought the watch but the manager merely shrugged his shoulders and suggested that next time Simon should look around *before* he spent his money.

Other price comparisons

Various other types of price comparison are also banned under the Bargain Offers Order 1979. These include:

- vague claims which suggest that the product is worth more than its selling price, such as 'Value £25, our price £14.99'
- vague comparisons with other traders' prices such as 'Our price £130, elsewhere £150' or 'Save £20 on department store prices'. But comparisons where the other trader is identified by name – such as 'Our price £45, price at Highprice Stores £55' – are allowed.

There are other price comparisons you should take with a pinch of salt:

- the use of insurance valuations on jewellery as a way of showing the piece is worth more than its selling price
- notices that say 'special offer' or 'star price' which suggest you are getting a bargain but do not mention a higher price at which the goods have been sold
- slogans which suggest in general terms that the shop's prices are low. Shops in the West End of London have been known to carry notices announcing a 'Closing down sale' for months or even years
- introductory offers which indicate that the price will rise after a certain date. In practice the goods may have been brought in for the sale and may be withdrawn, if unsold, on the quoted date, so that they are never actually on offer at the higher price.

Of course, some price comparisons are completely genuine. When you see a notice saying 'Previous price £135, now £109.99' or '£60. £45' the item should have been on sale in that shop at the higher price for at least 28 consecutive days in the previous six months; otherwise the trader is in breach of the Trade Descriptions Act 1968. However, the shop can display a disclaimer notice saying that the goods marked as reduced have not in fact been on sale in that shop for the specified period at the higher price or have been on sale in another branch of the same store – possibly several hundred miles away – at the higher price

Remember!

☞ If you see any sort of price comparison, the best advice is to ignore the apparent reduction and concentrate on the actual price at which the goods are being sold. Ask yourself if this represents value for money and compares favourably with prices in other shops.

Changes in the law

There are plans to tighten up the law on price comparisons. Under the Consumer Protection Bill, a statutory code of practice will be drawn up making it clear which kinds of price comparison are allowed and which are not. The aim is to prohibit any information about prices which is false or misleading. The new law is expected to say that:

- When a trader uses phrases like 'usual price', 'normal price', or 'reduced from', the higher price he quotes should be his own previous price. This should be the last price at which he offered the goods and one he used for at least 28 consecutive days in the previous six months.

- A trader can claim to have reduced an item from a higher previous price even if that item has never been on sale in that particular branch of his store before, as long as it has been on sale at the higher price in at least half of his other branches.

- A trader should not run an 'introductory offer' quoting a higher future price unless he intends to sell the goods at the higher price for at least 28 days in the three months after the introductory offer ends.

- If a trader compares the price of kit furniture with the ready-assembled price, he must have the ready-assembled version available for sale, or another named trader must have it available at the quoted price.

- The bans on 'manufacturer's recommended prices', 'recommended retail prices' and 'suggested selling prices' for certain types of goods will remain (see above) and other categories may be added to the list. Traders should not collude with manufacturers in the use of inflated recommended prices. Generally initials should not be used, but RRP can be used to indicate a recommended retail price.

- If a trader has only a limited number of items available in a particular line at the price he is quoting or is offering a bargain price on only a few colours in the range, he should make this clear in the price display.

How prices are displayed

Not all that long ago the only way to find out how much something cost was to ask the shopkeeper. Today, the law says that the prices of certain kinds of goods (mainly foods) must be on display, so saving shoppers time and embarrassment.

The price of food and drink sold in shops and from market stalls, mobile vans and street traders must be clearly displayed. The trader can choose whether to mark the price individually on each item, on the shelf, or by displaying a price list. There are exemptions for food sold by counter service – for example in a small corner shop, at the bakers and in counter service sections of supermarkets – and for food brought to the door – on a milk float, for instance, or a bread van. Food sold for consumption on the premises is also exempt. There are separate rules for restaurants (see Chapter 8).

There is also legislation covering petrol prices. The price per litre or per gallon must be shown at the pump; if the petrol is sold in litres the price per gallon must also be given. Filling stations do not have to have a roadside sign, but if they do it must give the cash price of four-star petrol, or the highest grade available, and must be clearly visible to approaching drivers. If there are any special conditions attached to the price – for example that it applies only to whole gallons or to orders over two gallons – then the roadside sign must make this clear.

Prices of other kinds of goods do not have to be displayed.

Fresh food

So that you can compare prices easily, the price of meat and fish per pound – the unit price – must be displayed wherever it is sold. If a piece of meat is prepacked and marked with its weight, the price of the whole piece must be given as well as the unit price. This applies to the most common kinds of fresh fish too, including cod, haddock, plaice and herring. But the rule does not apply to fish fingers or fish cakes.

Slightly different rules cover the sale of fresh fruit and vegetables. When these are prepacked, the price of the pack must be shown. When they are sold loose, a unit price per pound or per item must be given. Fruits and vegetables that can easily be counted can be sold by weight or per item.

The most common cheeses, including Cheddar, Cheshire, Edam and Gouda, must be marked with their price per pound.

VAT and other extras

When the price of a product is advertised or quoted, you can assume that this includes VAT unless the trader makes it clear that prices are exclusive of VAT. A shopkeeper cannot advertise one price and then tag the VAT on as an extra when you come to pay. If there are any other additional charges like postage and packing, you must be told about these in advance too.

Weights and measures

Another way in which comparing prices has been made easier is the introduction of standard packaging for certain items.

Most prepacked foods such as butter and margarine,

tea, instant coffee, sugar and flour can only be sold in packs of certain metric weights.

Many drinks available in pubs must also be sold in prescribed quantities when taken from a bottle or barrel. Beer and cider must be sold in thirds or half pints or multiples of a half pint. Gin, whisky, rum and vodka must be sold in measures of a quarter, a fifth or a sixth of a gill (a quarter pint).

There are no such rules covering the sale of wine by the glass. The size of glass used and the amount of wine in it depend entirely on the whim of the landlord. This makes it difficult to compare prices in different establishments. There is a voluntary code of practice which states that certain standard sizes of wine glass will be used and the quantity and price will be clearly displayed. Landlords do not have to stick to this code however, and recent surveys have shown that staff in many bars and restaurants do not even know of its existence.

It is an offence under the Weights and Measures Acts for a trader to sell you short weight or measure. If you think you have been given short weight, go back to the shop and ask for your money back. If you think the matter should be investigated further, tell the trading standards or consumer protection department at your local council offices.

Deciding to Buy

When you buy something you enter into a contract. The contract exists from the moment you offer to buy a particular item and the shopkeeper accepts your offer – you do not have to have paid any money, nor does the shopkeeper have to have given you a receipt. And, unless you are buying a house or flat, the contract does not have to be in writing. Once the contract is made, both you and the shopkeeper have certain responsibilities: he has to supply you with goods which comply with the law, and you have to pay for them.

A trader does not have to sell you the goods he has on display. By displaying them he is giving you an 'invitation to treat': he does not have to part with them.

Among other things, this means you cannot insist that a shopkeeper takes something out of the window to sell to you.

However, if the trader does agree to a sale, he must charge you the price at which the goods have been advertised or less.

Alec Smart was passing the window of his local electrical shop when he noticed an iron that normally sold for around £22 had been marked £12. When he asked to buy it, the sales assistant told him there had been a mistake and asked £22. Alec left the shop and reported the incident to the trading standards department at his local council offices. The shop had committed an offence under the Trade Descriptions Act 1968. The shop should have sold the iron to Alec for £12 or less, refused to sell it at all or changed the price ticket and then sold it to Alec for the full price.

It is perfectly legal for a shop to reprice goods on its shelves. If the same article is labelled with two prices, then the lowest one applies.

Ordering goods
Once you have agreed a price with a trader, he cannot ask you to pay more. If you order something and are quoted a price for it, that is what you will pay when it is delivered. The shopkeeper cannot ask you for more, even if the wholesale price goes up in the meantime. Of course it is wise to keep written proof of the agreed price when you order something.

If you will be expected to pay what the goods cost when they are delivered, rather than when they were ordered, then the shopkeeper must make this clear to you when you place your order. He may explain this to you himself, or the order form may say something like 'subject to price at time of delivery'.

If there is an increase in the rate of VAT between the

time of ordering and delivery, you will have to pay that increase.

Delivery dates

Sadly, most of us know what it is like to order goods on the promise that they'll be delivered 'in two or three weeks' and still to be waiting three months later. If it is important to you that your purchase arrives by a certain date, make this clear – preferably in writing – when you place your order. A note on the order form saying 'to be delivered by . . .' will suffice. If the item does not arrive by the specified date, the trader is in breach of contract and you can, if you choose, cancel your order and ask for the return of any deposit you have paid. You can also claim damages for any costs you have incurred as a result of the goods not arriving on time: for example the cost of buying a substitute at the last minute.

Even if you do not specify a delivery date, your goods should still arrive within a reasonable time. Try to find out how long delivery is likely to take when you place your order. When you feel you have waited long enough, contact the retailer and explain that the goods must be delivered by a certain date (you must give him a reasonable time – three or four weeks would be enough in most cases) and that if they do not arrive by then you will no longer require them and will ask for your deposit back. Confirm your conversation in writing. This is called making 'time of the essence of the contract'. If the goods have not arrived by the specified time, you are entitled to cancel the contract.

Deposits

Except in circumstances like those described above or when the trader cannot supply the goods you have ordered, you are not entitled to your deposit back. You cannot ask for it to be returned simply because you have changed your mind, however good your reason for doing so. In fact, if your change of heart involves the trader in more expense than is covered by the deposit – perhaps because he's made something specially for you which he cannot sell to anybody else – you may be asked to pay damages, which could be as much as the full price of the goods. So do think carefully before you order anything.

When the goods arrive
When your order arrives, you will probably be asked to sign a delivery note as proof that you have received it. Sometimes these notes include a clause stating that you agree that the item has arrived in good condition. If you have time, inspect the goods thoroughly there and then. If not, write 'goods not examined' alongside your signature. Otherwise you may have problems if the item does turn out to be faulty.

Buying Food and Groceries
It is a fact of life that, while many of us are prepared to spend time shopping around for electrical appliances, furniture and clothes, when it comes to groceries we prefer to find a supermarket whose premises, products and prices we like and to stick to it. As you probably spend more time and money in the supermarket over a year than you do in any other kind of shop, it is worth remembering that:

* For groceries, a supermarket or superstore is usually the cheapest. But bear in mind travelling costs when you compare prices with small self-service stores and counter service shops nearer your home.

* Some chains may have lower prices at their big superstores than at their high street branches. But once again, remember petrol costs.

* Supermarkets are not always cheapest for fresh produce but because you select your own food you have more control over quality.

* If poor parking facilities, narrow aisles and long queues make shopping a nightmare, you should ask yourself

whether the savings you are making are worth the hassle.

When you actually do your shopping remember that:

* You will usually save money by buying 'own brand' goods in a supermarket. Although these are often made by the manufacturers of the familiar branded varieties, quality and taste may vary. If you need to use far more 'own brand' soap powder in your wash than you do of the famous name brand, you may not be saving money.

* 'Money off' offers don't always mean big savings. Coffee with '10p off Manufacturer's Recommended Price' will not save you any money if the supermarket always sells that brand at 17p below the MRP anyway. Look at the price at which the goods are actually selling, rather than at colourful stickers and slogans.

* It's bad housekeeping to buy items you do not really want or need just because they carry special offers. On the other hand, be prepared to switch brands for a while to take advantage of a special offer if you think you will use your purchase.

Bulk buying
You can often save money by buying in bulk, either as an individual – negotiating special terms with your butcher for a large freezer order for example – or by joining forces with others and buying as a group. You can bulk buy at:

● cash and carry warehouses. Some welcome the public; others are open to traders and other special categories only. Before you spend a fortune, compare prices with own brand products at your local supermarket
● wholesale fruit and vegetable markets. Once again, many of these do not welcome members of the public, but if you belong to a bulk buy group and shop regularly, you may be able to find a wholesaler who will serve you

- quayside fish traders
- butchers and fishmongers
- freezer centres
- wholefood wholesalers.

A bulk buy group can be as large or as small, as sophisticated or as simple as you choose to make it. Some large groups have 100 or more members and operate a system where duty shoppers buy weekly and put the goods on display for their members to choose what they want. At the other end of the scale, a dozen friends take it in turns to buy once a month from a wholefood wholesaler. However modest the group, it does involve a good deal of organisation in taking orders, doing the shopping, weighing out and pricing each person's purchases from the bulk packs, distributing the goods and collecting the money.

Labelling

As anybody who buys groceries will have noticed, we are now given more information about the food we eat than ever before. But unless you know how to interpret the different terms, signs and symbols used on packets you could just end up confused. For example, what exactly does 'low calorie' mean and what is in a 'high fibre' cereal?

WHAT'S ON A LABEL

Ingredients. The label on almost all prepacked foods must list the ingredients in descending order of weight, including water if this makes up more than 5 per cent of the weight of the finished product. The list won't tell you how *much* sugar, flour or fat is in what you buy, but it will give you a clue to the relative proportions in the product. Virtually all additives must be listed too: you will usually see the additive's category – for cxample, preservative, flavour enhancer or colouring – and its chemical name or serial number.

Weight. With a few exceptions, the weight or volume of prepacked food must be shown on the label.

Datemarks. Most food must carry a datemark showing the date by which the food should be eaten – or, in the case of perishable foods, sold – to be enjoyed at its best. Foods which will last more than 18 months, deep frozen foods and fresh fruits and vegetables which have not been peeled or cut in pieces are among the foods which do not have to bear a datemark. A shopkeeper who sells a product outside the datemark is not committing an offence as long as the food is fit for human consumption and it is clear that the datemark has expired.

Producer's name. The label must also show the name of the food and the name and address of the manufacturer or packer or of a seller within the Common Market.

Fat content. At the time of writing the government is planning to introduce compulsory fat content labelling of food as recommended by the COMA report on Diet and Cardiovascular Disease.

Nutrition information. Some manufacturers and retail chains are choosing to give much more information than they are obliged to by law about the nutritional content of their foods, including the proportion of fat, carbohydrate, protein, fibre and sometimes salt and sugar. At the time of writing, the government is planning to introduce guidelines setting out a standard format for nutrition labelling so that it is easier for shoppers to compare different brands. The guidelines will be voluntary, though most companies are likely to follow them.

CLAIMS – WHAT THEY MEAN

To prevent the public being misled, the law puts some controls on the claims a food manufacturer can make for his product.

Calories. A maker cannot claim his food has a reduced energy value or is low in calories unless it fulfils certain conditions. If the word 'reduced' appears on the label, the food must not have more than three-quarters of the energy value of a similar food which makes no such claim. A 'low calorie' product must have no more than 40 kilocalories per 100 grams.

Protein. If a food is described as being 'high in protein', the amount of the product you would normally eat in a day must give you at least 12 grams of protein.

Vitamins. If a food is promoted as 'vitamin rich', the amount you would normally eat in a day must give you at least half the recommended daily dose of two or more specified vitamins.

Polyunsaturated fats. If a food carries a label saying it is high in polyunsaturates, its total fat content must be made up of at least 45 per cent polyunsaturated fat and no more than 25 per cent saturated fat. At least 35 per cent of the product by weight must be fat of some kind and the label must make clear the amount of each type of fat it contains.

Sugar. Jam, fruit jelly or marmalade labelled 'low' or 'reduced' sugar must have less sugar than the usual kind of preserve. But there are no other controls over the uses of the phrases 'low' or 'reduced' in reference to sugar, so in practice they may mean very little. Of course if a product is described as 'sugar free' then it must contain no added sugar; but this does not necessarily mean it has fewer calories. One way in which manufacturers try to disguise the amount of sugar in their products is to break it up in the list of ingredients into its different chemical constituents. So instead of seeing the word 'sugar' near the top of the list (which would indicate it is a major ingredient), you might see 'sucrose', 'maltose', 'dextrose', 'honey', 'molasses' and 'corn syrup' all listed separately. Don't be misled – they are all bad for your teeth and your figure.

Other claims. The Ministry of Agriculture, Fisheries and Food is working on definitions of the words 'high' and 'low' in the context of food labelling. At present there are controls on the use of these words only when they apply to the categories of food described above. So, if you see them in any other context, treat the claim with scepticism. If a product is described as containing 'extra' or 'more' of some ingredient – like butter in a biscuit or fruit in a flan – then the manufacturer must state on the label what percentage of that emphasised ingredient his product contains.

MISLEADING LABELS
The name of a food must not mislead you. If you see a carton of yoghurt with pictures of raspberries on it or labelled 'raspberry yoghurt' or 'raspberry flavoured' yoghurt, then its flavour must come from real raspberries. If it is labelled 'raspberry flavour', you can assume its flavour does not come mainly from the fruit.

If there is a picture on the packet, it should be a fair representation of what is inside. This applies to written descriptions on packets too. If you have been misled by packaging and feel that the product does not match its description, contact the trading standards department at your local council offices: the company may have committed an offence under the Trade Descriptions Act 1968 and/or the Food Act 1984.

Meat and fish products
If you buy a processed meat product like a tinned meat pie or a beefburger, you may find it reassuring to know that the government lays down the minimum proportion of meat this must contain. But the amount may not be as high as you thought: a beef sausage might contain just 25 per cent beef; and a fish finger could in theory have as little as 15 per cent fish, though in practice most contain 50 per cent or more. These are the minimum meat and fish contents of some of the most popular varieties:

Burger – 80 per cent; a beefburger must be at least 80 per cent beef
Economy burger – 60 per cent

Luncheon meat – 85 per cent
Meat paste or paté – 70 per cent
Pork sausage – 65 per cent, of which 80 per cent must be pork
Beef sausage – 50 per cent, of which half must be beef
Meat pie – 25 per cent
Cooked meat and vegetable pie – 12½ per cent
Fish fingers – no minimum.

In the case of meat pies, sausages and patés, at least half the meat content must be lean meat – i.e. free from fat. In the case of burgers, at least 65 per cent of the meat must be lean. If water has been added to cured meat, the water content must be clearly marked. And if a product which looks as if it consists entirely of meat actually contains other ingredients, these must be named too.

Bad food
If you have bought food which is 'off' or contains something which should not be there, take it back to the shop and ask for your money back. If you think the matter should be investigated further, contact the environmental health officer at your local council offices as soon as possible. Obviously he will want to see a sample of the food.

2

Buying away from a Shop

You can buy not only in the high street but in your own home, or somebody else's. You can shop by post from catalogues and newspapers. You can even order by telephone. And if you like getting out but can't face the shops, you can visit markets and special sales.

All this adds spice to shopping, but it has its snags too. If you are used to buying from a shop, you may find it more difficult to think clearly and make sensible decisions in a different environment. As a result, you could end up buying something you would not normally touch in a department store.

For this reason it is especially important to think carefully before you buy away from a shop and to know exactly what your rights are.

Buying on Your Doorstep

Most of us have had a visit from a doorstep salesman at some time. If he's reputable – and most are – he will identify himself straight away and tell you what he is selling. If he's not, he may not reveal that he's actually selling anything until he has gained your confidence. The Office of Fair Trading publishes a useful leaflet

How to Cope with Doorstep Salesmen which describes some of the tricks of the trade and how to resist them.

Beware of people who claim to be safety consultants or security advisers: they'll convince you that your home is a fire trap or a burglar's paradise and then try to sell you a fire extinguisher or a burglar alarm. Other salesmen will ask if you'd like to cut your fuel bills and then try to sell you insulation or replacement windows. Then there are those who claim to be conducting market research: you start by 'answering a few questions' and before you know it, you're looking at a set of encyclopaedias. Some salesmen claim they're working on behalf of the disabled, the unemployed or a charity. If they're genuine, they'll be happy to show you proof of identity. But not many real charities sell this way: all too often the goods are highly priced and badly made and the money goes straight into the seller's pocket. Finally, steer clear of the workman who 'just happens to be passing' and couldn't help noticing that you had a few slates missing or that your chimney looked a bit dodgy. His trick is to panic you into agreeing to a quick, expensive and possibly totally unnecessary piece of work. And if he botches it, you may find him strangely hard to trace.

The sales techniques

You will find it easier to resist the pressures of doorstep salesmen if you know how they work. The reputable ones will take 'no' for an answer and will go away if you are firm. But sales representatives are adept at spotting potential customers: their living depends on it. They know that many householders, caught off guard and confronted with a winning smile and a barrage of carefully prepared patter, will buy something just to get rid of them or because they are too embarrassed to say 'no' and shut the door. They can also recognise a waverer when they see one. Generally speaking, the more expensive the item being sold, the more time the salesman is prepared to invest in trying to talk you round. Reps selling double glazing, home extensions and the like have been known to spend hours with potential customers in the hope that they'll ultimately make a sale. Their ploys include:

* the 'showhouse' technique. You'll be flattered to be told your home has been selected as a showhouse for the company's product – a loft conversion perhaps or 'all weather' cladding. In return you are promised a 'special price' for the work. You may feel less flattered when you discover that the same offer has been made to all your neighbours.

* the 'sign tonight' discount. You'll be told that if the salesman can avoid calling back, it keeps the cost down and the saving is passed on to you, the customer.

* the 'buy now before prices rise' offer. Prices always seem to be going up 'next week': another ruse to get you to make a quick decision.

* the 'I'll lose my job if I don't get this order' story. Yes, salesmen have been known to use emotional blackmail in order to secure a sale. The customer who has spent an evening with the rep is made to feel that he is stabbing a friend in the back if he doesn't sign on the dotted line.

Simon Simple opened his door to a couple of men who said they were doing some work 'for the council' in the next road and noticed his drive looked a bit rough. They gave him a competitive quote for re-laying it and Simon agreed to the work. At first the new drive looked splendid, but within a week it began to break up. Simon rang the number on the scrap of paper the men had given him, but it turned out to be a betting shop. He told the trading standards department at his local council offices but the men were never traced. The following year Simon called in a firm of local builders to re-lay the drive again.

How to buy wisely
If you buy sensibly and from reputable traders, door-

step shopping can be a useful alternative to the high street. But do follow the 'buy-laws':

☞ As soon as you know that you do not want or cannot afford what the salesman is offering, say 'no thanks' and shut the door. Otherwise you will just waste everybody's time or, worse, end up with something you do not really want.

☞ Find out whom the seller represents and why he is calling. Ask for identification and scrutinise it carefully: a rogue will try to get away with flashing a bogus card before your eyes. People who sell or collect door-to-door on behalf of a charity need a licence from the local authority. For security reasons, don't let a stranger into your home if you are alone. If in doubt, phone the number on the trader's business card or ask him to return later when you will have somebody else with you.

☞ Don't let yourself be pressurised. Ask yourself whether you really want and need what's on offer and if so, why. If you are uncertain, discuss the matter with the salesman. But remember, he'll have an answer to every objection: that's his job.

☞ Never sign anything on the spot or agree to have work done straight away, no matter how alluring the incentives for placing an immediate order. If after careful thought and a night's sleep, you still want the goods, the salesman will still be delighted to hear from you and you may still be able to negotiate a discount. If you buy on credit or from a member of certain trade associations, you have a 'cooling off-period' during which you can change your mind (see below, page 27). In theory, you could take advantage of this to do some hard thinking and shopping around. In practice – as the salesman very well knows – you are unlikely to cancel your order once you have signed.

☞ Shop around and compare prices before you buy, as you would if you were in the high street. Don't buy anything unless you are satisfied it is good value. Before you agree to home improvements, get at least two other estimates for the work.

☞ If you are buying on credit, find out what the total cost will be and compare this with the cost of credit from other sources.

☞ Make sure you know what you are buying. It is surprising how many people are disappointed because the goods they've ordered do not match up to the salesman's colourful description. Ask to see pictures and if possible samples of what is available. If you are buying a home improvement ask to see other houses in your area where the company has done work. If the salesman makes big promises which tempt you, check with his company – preferably by letter – that the product will do all he says. (For more detail on how to choose a firm to carry out home improvements, see Chapter 5, pages 90–4.)

☞ Make sure you know how much you are spending. If you are buying something like a set of books which will arrive by instalments over a long period, work out the total cost.

☞ Never sign anything unless you have read it carefully and understand what it says. If in doubt, seek advice from a consumer advice centre or citizens' advice bureau. Ignore offers from the salesman to complete the form himself 'to save you time'.

☞ Don't pay the whole sum in advance. If you hand over a deposit, get a proper receipt on headed notepaper with the firm's name, address and phone number.

☞ If you do buy anything, make sure you know how to contact the salesman again. If things go wrong, you will need to be able to reach the person who sold you the goods.

Your rights

If there is something wrong with a product you have bought, you have the same rights as if you had made your purchase in a shop (see Chapter 3). If you have had a service performed, such as the installation of central heating or double glazing, you are protected by different legislation (see Chapter 5).

Changing your mind
Generally speaking, you cannot expect your money back simply because you have changed your mind after you have bought something. However, if you pay for something at home by credit, you do have the right to cancel, if you do so within five days. In order to qualify for this cooling-off period, you must have signed the credit agreement at home after discussing the arrangement with the trader in person. (For more detail on credit see Chapter 11.)

If you take out a long-term life assurance policy at home, you also have a cooling-off period – in this case ten days.

Certain trade associations whose members are involved in doorstep selling have drawn up codes of practice which allow consumers a cooling-off period. These include the Glass and Glazing Federation, which represents many of the major double glazing companies, and the Direct Selling Association (DSA).

By the end of 1987, there will be new legislation to protect you when you buy on the doorstep. You will have a seven-day cooling-off period when you buy from a trader who calls at your home or work without making an appointment. This won't apply to:

- transactions worth less than about £35
- visits by regular roundsmen such as milkmen
- agency mail order shopping
- contracts for home extensions; but it will apply to home improvements.

Buying by Telephone
In America, telephone sales are big business, with all manner of goods and services being ordered and paid for down the line. In Britain, this form of selling is still in its infancy. But it is growing.

At present, companies that use the telephone generally do so to arrange for a representative to call or in response to a consumer's request for more information: insurance companies and home improvement firms seem to favour this approach. The main criticisms of this type of call are that they are a nuisance and that the callers do not always make their purpose clear until the conversation is well under way.

However, the number of companies actually using the telephone to *sell* their products is increasing. If you agree to buy something, you could find yourself entering into a legally binding contract without having a clear idea of what you have ordered. The Office of Fair Trading has drawn up a series of guidelines on telephone selling. Among other things, these say that:

- You should not receive personal phonecalls at your place of work.
- Callers should say who they are, what company they are representing and why they are telephoning. They should not be evasive or misleading.
- Callers should ask whether the timing is convenient.
- Consumers who order goods during an unsolicited phonecall should be given at least seven days' cooling-off period in which to change their minds.

These guidelines are purely voluntary. So if you do receive an unexpected sales call:

* Try to find out the purpose of the call quickly.

* Be wary of people claiming to conduct market research on the telephone.

* Don't agree to buy anything unless you are allowed a cooling-off period.

* If you are continually bothered by calls you don't want from one company, take their name and address and write a letter of complaint. If you have no success, contact the British Direct Marketing Association (BDMA), which represents many of the major com-

panies involved in this field, and which will follow up
complaints like this, even against non-members.

Buying at a Party

This is another variation on the 'buying in the comfort
of home' theme – only in this case the home is not
generally your own. While you relax over coffee at a
friend's house, an agent demonstrates her products
and invites you to try and buy. Orders are taken and the
goods are delivered later.

As a method of selling, it is immensely successful.
Only one person in five leaves a selling party without
making at least one purchase. Its advantages are obvious. The surroundings are more comfortable and the
atmosphere more relaxed than in a shop and the
demonstrator has more time to discuss and describe
her wares than shop assistants generally have; and if
you buy from a member of the Direct Selling Association, which represents most party plan companies, you
have a cooling-off period of 14 days in which to return
what you have bought if you decide you do not want it.

The main drawback of party selling is that you may
buy because you don't want to look mean or be the odd
one out or because you know that the size of the gift
your hostess receives at the end of the party depends on
how much money has been taken.

Problems can also arise if the agent does not represent a reputable company. There are sharks who
operate an unsavoury practice known as 'switch selling', usually involving jewellery. Partygoers are shown
a range of attractive pieces, place their orders and hand
over their money. When the goods arrive, they are
vastly inferior to the range demonstrated.

If you go to a selling party, follow the 'buy-laws':

☞   Don't feel obliged to buy just because everybody else
     seems to be doing so.

☞   Don't pay until you receive the goods.

☞   Find out what happens if, once the goods arrive, you decide you do not like them, or – in the case of clothes – they do not fit you. Can you return them?

☞   If you stick to parties run by members of the DSA, you have the protection of a code of practice backed by the Office of Fair Trading. The association also operates a conciliation procedure for complaints against member companies.

☞   Always make a note of the name and address of the company and its local agent so you know who to complain to if things go wrong.

The Friendly Approach

Some companies that sell direct – that is, not from business premises – have a different style. They rely on agents to contact everybody they know – friends, relatives, neighbours, business colleagues – and to try to sell them products or services from their range.

If somebody asks you to buy products in this way, such as cosmetics, health-care products or household cleaners, try to compare prices and quality with what is available in the shops. If you are asked to buy a service, such as insurance, get quotes from other companies too. Do not feel you have to buy just because the salesman is a friend or acquaintance who stands to make a commission from your purchase.

Buying by Mail Order

Mail order shopping offers you all the advantages of buying at home without the pressure of dealing with a salesman. However, there are points to remember if you want to get the best deal and – with some kinds of mail order in particular – avoid pitfalls for the unwary.

Buying from a catalogue

You are well protected when you buy from a catalogue published by one of the large mail order companies because all the big names in this field belong to the Mail

Order Traders' Association (MOTA) which has drawn up a code of practice backed by the Office of Fair Trading. This code appears to work fairly well. It says that:

- The cash price of the goods, including VAT, must be clearly printed in the catalogue.
- It must be clear whether postage, packing and delivery costs are included and, if not, what these are. If there is an extra delivery charge for your part of the country, you will be told.
- You are allowed to examine the goods on approval – usually for at least a couple of weeks – before deciding whether to keep them. If you return them, any money you've paid will be refunded. Under the code, firms are not obliged to pay your postage costs, but all MOTA members do.
- If the goods are faulty or damaged in transit, you can return them and get a refund.
- If what you have ordered is not available, the company may send a substitute rather than disappoint you. But you can return it if you do not like it.
- You should be told if any goods come in kit form.
- If there is an undue delay in delivery, you should be told. If you have been given a delivery date and the goods do not arrive by then, you can cancel your order and ask for a refund of any money you have paid.
- There will be servicing facilities for goods which need them.
- The catalogue must tell you what to do if you have a complaint.

If you buy from a catalogue company which does not belong to MOTA, check the points outlined above before you place your order.

Buying from book and record clubs
No doubt you have seen those alluring advertisements offering books or records at a fraction of their normal price. In return for taking advantage of these savings, you commit yourself to ordering a certain number of

items over the following year. Many companies which offer this kind of deal belong to the Mail Order Publishers' Authority (MOPA) which has also agreed a code of practice with the Office of Fair Trading. The code says that:

- Companies will spell out in their advertisements the main points of their special offers and any strings attached. If there are postage and packing charges, this will be made clear.
- If goods are offered on 'free approval', the company will pay the cost of return postage.
- You may cancel once you have bought the agreed number of items and before this if prices rise more than you could 'reasonably have anticipated'.
- If delivery is unduly delayed, you should be told and given a chance to cancel your order.
- Companies should constantly review their methods of billing and collecting payments so that members are not bothered by letters asking for money they have already paid.

If you do join a book or record club, read the terms and conditions carefully, so you know what you will be expected to buy. Some clubs send you the 'choice of the month' (or quarter) unless you let them know that you do not want it. If you are the kind of person who puts off making decisions, you may find yourself buying items you do not really want, simply because you did not get round to posting the refusal letter.

When you join most clubs, you undertake to buy a certain number of items in the first year, after which you can cancel. In some cases the commitment is for longer: check before you sign. If you try to cancel before you have bought the agreed number of books or records, you will probably be asked to pay the full cost of the special offer items you received when you joined, or to return them in good condition.

If you have a complaint about a book or record club, write to the Director of MOPA outlining the problem.

Buying from an advertisement

Every newspaper and magazine carries advertisements for goods you can order by post – clothes, furniture, gifts, personal horoscopes and manuals on how to be a success in the betting shop, the boardroom and even in bed. The vast majority of people who buy goods this way are delighted with their purchases and get their money back if they are not. But some are disappointed and some are, frankly, conned.

The British Code of Advertising Practice, operated by the Advertising Standards Authority (ASA), has rules covering advertisements which ask customers to send cash with their order. The code says that:

- The advertiser should say how long delivery will take – the period should not be longer than 28 days. If he cannot meet the deadline, he should let you know when the order will arrive and give you an opportunity to cancel. Plants and made-to-measure goods are exempt from the 28-day delivery rule.
- You can ask for a refund:

  – if the goods do not arrive within the promised time
  – if the advertisement offers a 'money back guarantee'
  – if you return the goods, undamaged, within seven working days of receiving them
  – when the goods are faulty or do not match their description; in this case you can also claim return postage.

- Advertisers should give a refund – not a credit note, unless you ask for one – as soon as they receive your request for payment.

If you come across an advertisement which seems to breach the code, let the ASA know. The Authority will take the matter up with the trader and can ask newspapers and magazines not to carry his advertisements.

The British Direct Marketing Association (BDMA) has its own code of practice, with rules on the subject of selling through advertisements that overlap with those of the ASA. If you have a complaint against a member company and cannot resolve it with the firm itself, the BDMA will investigate.

Alec Smart ordered a set of towels from an advertisement in a Sunday paper. He intended to give them as a present to a friend who was getting married six weeks later. The ad promised delivery within 21 days. After a month Alec had heard nothing, so he wrote to the company explaining that if the towels did not arrive within seven days, he would consider that the company had broken its contract and would ask for his money back. A week later he had still heard nothing, so he wrote again, asking for a refund, and threatening to report the company to the ASA. He received a cheque by return of post.

If you lose your money

The main danger when you send off payment in advance for something you have seen in an advertisement is that the company may go out of business before your goods are dispatched or that you may be dealing with a rogue who simply takes your money and runs. Every year about £4 million is lost this way. That is a tiny proportion of the total amount sent in response to cash-with-order adverts, but it is still a great deal of money.

You do have some protection when you buy from a newspaper or magazine advertisement. The five main associations of newspaper and magazine publishers operate Mail Order Protection Schemes (MOPS). Under the MOPS, you are entitled to a refund if you have sent money in advance to an advertiser who goes bankrupt or into liquidation. However, it is thought that only 7 per cent of advertisements that ask you to send cash with your order are actually covered by these schemes, which makes their value limited. You are not protected if you send money:

- in response to a classified advertisement
- after you receive a catalogue from an advertiser
- in response to advertisements in publications which do not belong to a MOPS – this includes many of the smaller specialist magazines.

Only the scheme run by the Newspaper Publishers' Association covers money sent in response to an insert inside a publication. This is also the only one which protects you if the trader simply disappears with your money. The others are obliged to pay out only if the trader has gone bankrupt or into liquidation, though they will sometimes make special payments in other cases.

If you have sent money to an advertiser and hear nothing after 28 days, try to contact the trader direct to find out what has happened. If you have no success, write immediately to the advertising manager of the newspaper or magazine concerned telling him:

* the date of the advertisement

* what you ordered

* when you ordered it

* what you paid and how

* your name and address

* any other information which may be useful.

If you are entitled to a refund, you will be told and must put in a formal claim within two months of your order if the advertisement was in a magazine and within three months of the date of the newspaper if it was in a paper. If you do not have a claim under a MOPS, contact the trading standards department in the area where the trader has his business. They may be able to tell you what has happened.

How to protect yourself
When you buy by mail order of any kind, follow the 'buy-laws':

☞ If you are replying to an advertisement, keep details of when and where it appeared and if possible keep a copy of the ad itself.

☞ Never send cash through the post.

☞ If you pay by cheque or postal order, keep your stubs or counterfoils.

☞ If you pay by credit card for goods over £100, you have extra protection. In certain cases the card company must reimburse you if you lose money.

☞ If the goods do not arrive within the promised time, write to the company explaining that if they are not delivered within a specified period – say two or three weeks – you will cancel your order and ask for a refund. This is called *making time of the essence of the contract*.

☞ Keep copies of any correspondence you have with a mail order company and dated notes of any phonecalls.

☞ If you return any mail order goods, get a certificate of posting or a receipt from the carrier.

Unsolicited goods
If you receive goods through the post that you have not ordered – called unsolicited goods – and you do not want to keep them, you have two choices. You can write to the company which sent them, explaining that the goods were unsolicited and that you do not want them. The company then has 30 days in which to collect them. If nobody calls in that time, they are yours.

Alternatively, you can sit tight and do nothing. Keep the goods safely – do not use them – and if nobody calls within six months they are yours.

Ignore any letters demanding payment for un-solicited goods: the sender may be committing an offence under the Unsolicited Goods and Services Acts 1971 and 1975 and could be prosecuted.

Leaflets through the Post

If you are fed up with being deluged with offers through the post, you can ask for your name to be removed from the mailing lists of the major companies trading this way by writing to the Mailing Preference Service. You can also write to the MPS if you want *more* mail on particular subjects. A similar scheme is being devised for telephone sales calls.

Buying at Markets

Markets are good places to save money or – if you are not careful – to squander it. To play safe, stick to regular markets and regular stallholders – they generally have a proper stall with their name and address at the top and may even have printed carrier bags and receipts. Beware of 'fly pitchers' selling out of suitcases or from trailers or trestle tables: these are the people most likely to sell you rotten fruit, stolen goods, or cheap, nasty and even dangerous products. And they're also more likely to have disappeared without trace just when you want to complain about something you have bought.

When you shop at a market, make a note of the number of the stallholder's pitch and the day of the week on which you are buying. If something goes wrong with your purchase and you cannot trace the seller, contact the market superintendent at your local council offices. Market traders have to be licenced by the local authority and councils keep records of stall-holders' names and addresses.

Buying at One-day Sales

You've probably seen newspaper advertisements or had handouts stuffed through your letterbox promot-ing special one-day sales. The bargains promised are

certainly alluring, with special rewards for those who
come early. Some sales of this kind offer genuine value
for money. Others are nothing more than a con-trick.

Beware of sales conducted as mock-auctions. This is
where goods are sold to people at a price lower than
their highest bid; or where you can bid for certain
items only after you have agreed to buy others; or
where the salesman gives articles away or offers them
as gifts. Mock auctions are against the law and the
people who run them are out to make a quick financial
killing rather than to serve consumers.

Beware too of sales advertised by leaflets pushed
through your door which do not carry the name and
address of the sale organiser. If there is a phone number
printed, ring it and ask what time the sale starts. If you
get no reply, be on your guard. If you cannot trace the
organiser *before* the sale you are unlikely to be able to
find him afterwards, should you want to complain
about a purchase. If you do attend a one-day sale:

☞   Remember that the bargains featured in the advertise-
      ments at rock bottom prices may not actually be offered
      for sale; they are intended to draw the crowds.

☞   Ask to examine the goods before you buy. Sometimes
      the goods on display are of a higher quality than the
      ones actually sold.

☞   Don't be carried away by the apparently amazing bar-
      gains others seem to be snatching up. Rogue traders
      sometimes plant their friends among the crowd and
      'sell' them something for nothing in order to whet the
      appetites of genuine customers who may not get the
      same treatment. People have been known to pay £50 for
      a sealed package only to find once they'd left the sale
      that they had bought goods worth £5.

☞   Insist on a receipt when you buy something and
      take down the trader's name, address and telephone
      number.

3

When Things Go Wrong

When we shop, we expect our money's worth. We want what we buy to do what it is meant to do – to cut well if it is a knife, to write smoothly if it is a pen – and to stay in one piece for a reasonable length of time.

Unfortunately, some of us are going to be disappointed. However carefully we shop, few of us are lucky enough to be completely satisfied with everything we buy. Some products are badly made or poorly designed in ways we cannot foresee, or develop faults early on for no apparent reason. When that happens we are entitled to complain and to be compensated.

Few people enjoy complaining and many people do not bother because they lack the energy or the confidence, or both. But complaining is worthwhile – and not only because it may bring direct rewards like a refund, a replacement or a repair. It is only by being made aware of faults in their products that makers can improve their standards. As for shops, it is their duty to sort out complaints about faulty goods, and they should be given a chance to put matters right. If they deal with you fairly, they deserve to keep your custom. If they don't, you should go elsewhere.

How the Law Protects You

The law recognises that what you buy should be of a certain standard. When you offer to buy something and the seller accepts your offer, you are both entering into a contract which gives you certain rights and the seller certain responsibilities. The most important of these are enshrined in the Sale of Goods Act 1979. This says that **all** goods bought from a trader, no matter whether new or secondhand, whether purchased in a shop, at your home, in a market or by mail order, must be:

- **as described** – on the packaging and labelling, at the point of sale and by the seller. If you have chosen from a sample, what you buy must match that too. If you specifically ask for waterproof boots and are sold a fashion pair which turn to blotting paper in the first shower, they are not as described.
- **of merchantable quality.** This rather old-fashioned phrase means that what you buy should function properly and not be defective. If you buy a handbag and the strap snaps off for no obvious reason after you have used it twice, then it is not of merchantable quality.
- **reasonably fit for their purpose.** In other words, they must do what they are supposed to do. A new vacuum cleaner that did not pick up would not be fit for its purpose, nor would a fly spray that left the insects in perfect health. Supposing you ask for a product which will do something specific – a pair of scissors for cutting fabric, say – and the sales assistant assures you that the pair you have chosen will fit the bill. If it turns out that he has sold you paper scissors, the item is not fit for its intended purpose. But if the sales assistant had said he had no idea whether the scissors were suitable for dressmaking, or said they should only be used on paper, you would not be entitled to complain.

When You Should Complain

If what you have bought does not fulfil one or more of these three conditions, you may be entitled to a refund or compensation under the Sale of Goods Act. But you won't have a case if:

* you simply change your mind about something you have bought. If you buy a jumper and your husband does not like the colour or a new lampshade that just does not look right when it is up, the shopkeeper does not have to help you out of your fix. Some shops *are* willing to exchange goods which are unsuitable, provided they have not been used and you have proof of purchase. If the trader agrees before you buy something that he will exchange it or give you a refund in these circumstances, then he must stick by his word. If this is not the shop's normal policy, it is a good idea to ask the assistant to put the promise in writing on the receipt – otherwise you may have difficulty in proving it was made.

---

* you did the damage yourself.

---

* you were told about the defect before you bought the goods. If a dress is marked 'shop-soiled' you cannot demand a refund because it turns out to be grubbier than it looked under the store's lighting.

---

* you examined the article and should have seen the faults. If you examine something before you buy, give it a thorough inspection: otherwise you are better off not checking it at all.

---

* the goods were a present. In law, the contract is between the seller and the buyer. If the article is passed on to somebody else, that person has no rights under the Sale of Goods Act. In practice, however, many shops will help you out if you have been given a present which is faulty, provided they are satisfied that it was purchased from them. If you do not know where the goods were bought or the shop is unhelpful, you could contact the manufacturer or claim under the guarantee. Alternatively – and if this does not cause embarrassment – you could explain your problem to the person who gave you the present and ask them to sort it out for you.

If something you have purchased is faulty, go back to

the place where you bought it. Your contract is with the seller and it is he, not the manufacturer, who must deal with problems which arise.

Serious faults

Put simply, the more serious the defect and the sooner it appears, the stronger your case. If your new kettle does not boil or your cardigan shrinks to child-size on its first wash, the position is clear: you are entitled to reject the goods and ask for your money back. You do not have to accept a replacement or a repair. As soon as you discover the fault, you should stop using the goods; if you don't, you may forfeit your right to reject them. Contact the shop immediately – by phone if you cannot get there in person.

Minor faults

If the defect is relatively small – a scratch on the side of a fridge, or a dud light on a new car, say – you are not entitled to reject the goods and ask for a refund and you probably would not want to. In a case like this you would be entitled to compensation to make up the difference between what you paid for the goods and what they are actually worth with the fault. In practice this compensation may take the form of 'money off' – in the case of the fridge – or a free repair – in the case of the broken light. Problems can arise when the repair does not cure the fault or when further defects develop. That is why it is a good idea to reserve your right to reject under the Sale of Goods Act as described below (see page 45).

When faults develop later

The longer you have owned something, the weaker your case is for rejecting it and claiming a refund. So when you buy anything, examine it carefully as soon as you get it home and, where possible, try it out. You will not be able to reject a faulty kettle two years after you bought it even if you put it away as a spare and never used it.

But even if you are not entitled to a refund, you may be able to claim compensation. The courts have recognised that goods not only should be of merchantable quality when they are bought but should remain free of defects for a reasonable time. What is reasonable depends on the type of goods involved and to some extent on what you paid and are therefore entitled to expect. For example, you would expect a pair of expensive walking shoes to last longer and wear better than strappy fashion sandals; you might be prepared to write off a cheap hairdrier if you were told it was not worth repairing after two years' continuous use, but you would feel justifiably aggrieved if an engineer said the same thing about a cooker of similar age. The size of the fault will also affect your entitlement to compensation. It may be reasonable for the door catch on your tumble drier to need replacing after 18 months but not the motor.

If you think a fault has developed in an unreasonably short time, return to the shop without delay. Ask them either to repair the goods free of charge or to pay for the cost of repair by somebody else. If the goods cannot be mended, you may be entitled to compensation: the amount will depend on the age of the goods.

Extra Compensation

When you claim a refund or compensation because something you have bought is faulty, you can include additional expenses you have incurred such as postage or travel. You may also be able to claim the cost of hiring an alternative while yours is unusable. You may also be able to claim for any damage or injury caused because the goods were defective.

> Alec Smart bought a washing machine which flooded the kitchen, ruining the vinyl flooring, which was also new. Alec contacted the shop. They offered to replace the machine, but said he would

have to wait three weeks as they did not have that model in stock. Alec accepted their offer (he could have insisted on a refund as the machine was not of merchantable quality) and claimed from the shop the cost of replacing the flooring and of six visits to the launderette.

Your Rights
Sometimes you will be genuinely impressed by the way a shop deals with a problem concerning faulty goods. But research has shown that many consumers are unhappy with the way their complaints are handled. One survey, by the National Consumer Council, revealed that 85 per cent of those questioned were dissatisfied with the way a trader had dealt with their complaint. Below I describe how to present your complaint so that you have the best chance of success. It is also important to know your rights, so that you will not be fobbed off when you have a genuine grievance. Don't be deterred if the shopkeeper tells you:

* *that he cannot give you a refund because you have used the goods and he cannot resell them*. The answer to this one is that you could not tell that the goods were defective until you used them. Your rights depend on the size of the fault and how long you've had the goods (see above, page 42).

* *that the goods were perfect when they left the shop: you must have caused the damage*. This can be tricky as it may be your word against the shopkeeper's. Stand your ground if you know you are in the right. If you feel it is worthwhile, you could have the goods examined by an independent expert (see Chapter 13, page 264).

* *to contact the manufacturer*. In this case, remind him that the problem has nothing to do with the manufacturer: it is the shop's responsibility.

* *to use the guarantee*. Your reply could be the same as in

the case above. But if the defect is fairly minor, you may be happy to claim under the guarantee. It is up to you. (See below for some guidelines to help you decide when to use a guarantee.)

* *that he can do nothing because the guarantee has expired.* Your Sale of Goods Act rights are not affected when the guarantee runs out. If your washing machine needs a new motor or your car a new gearbox at 15 months, it is irrelevant that they are 'out of guarantee': if you were entitled to expect these parts to last longer, you could claim compensation from the seller.

* *that he will send the goods away to be repaired.* If you are basically happy with your purchase and the fault is small, you may decide to accept a repair. But if you think you are entitled to a refund and want one because you have completely lost confidence in the product, then stand firm. If you accept a repair, write to the shop explaining that although you are allowing them to attempt a repair you reserve your right under the Sale of Goods Act to reject the goods and ask for a refund if the repair is unsuccessful or if further faults develop.

* *that he will give you a credit note.* If you are happy with a credit note to be spent at the same shop (or any branch of the same chain), fine. But you do not have to accept one. Remember that if you do opt for a credit note, you cannot change your mind later and ask for cash if there is nothing in the shop that you want. And some credit notes have a time limit on them.

* *that he never gives refunds at sale time.* A shopkeeper who displays a notice saying 'no refunds given' is breaking the law. He cannot duck his responsibilities under the Sale of Goods Act.

* *that he never gives refunds without a receipt.* In law, you do not lose your rights because you do not have a receipt and a shopkeeper cannot insist you have one before he will consider your complaint. In practice, though, having proof of purchase can make things a

good deal easier and it is understandable that a shop should want some evidence that the goods were bought from them in the fairly recent past. If you do not have a receipt, a cheque stub or credit card counterfoil should suffice. Even though the law is on your side, you do have real problems if you have no proof of purchase at all and the trader is unwilling to listen to your complaint.

How to Complain Effectively
It may seem pessimistic to think about how you'll complain before you've even paid for your purchases. But there are precautions you can take *when you shop* which may help your case if something you buy turns out to be faulty.

☞ Always ask for a receipt and keep it either until you have stopped using the goods or until they are so old that you are unlikely to complain to the shop if a fault develops. Some till receipts are minute scraps of paper which do not even carry the name of the shop. When you get one of these, write the name of the shop and what you bought on the back before you file it away.

☞ If you shop when you are away from home, stick to chain stores. Complaining can be tricky if something goes wrong with your purchase and the shop is 200 miles away.

☞ If you want the goods for a specific purpose, explain this to the sales assistant. If you seek his advice and take it, make a note of what he said: this could help if he turns out to have given you wrong information.

If something you have bought is faulty:

* Stop using it as soon as you notice the defect and contact the seller, either in person or by telephone. Legally, the trader should collect faulty goods, but it is quicker to return them to the shop yourself and more likely to preserve goodwill.

* Decide beforehand what you want from the shop and what you will do if they refuse your request. You will create a better impression – and impressions can be all-important – if it is clear that you have thought the problem through and worked out what you think is a reasonable solution.

* Keep a diary of events – this can be useful as an *aide memoire* if you end up in court.

* When you visit the shop, take with you your receipt or some other proof of purchase. Ask to see the manager or the owner: there is no point wasting everybody's time complaining to a sales assistant who has no power to help you. Remain calm and put your case as clearly and concisely as possible. Refer to notes, if this helps. If you ask to see the manager in private, it will show that you are trying to be reasonable. Later you may feel a more public demonstration of your grievance would be appropriate.

  Tell the manager when you bought the goods and what is wrong with them and give him a chance to offer a solution. If he refuses to help you, it may be because he does not want to or because he does not have the power to deal with problems of this kind. **Do not give up.** If there is one quality you need when complaining, it is persistence. If you have a genuine grievance, persevere.

* Your next step is to write to the managing director at the head office – the shop manager should give you his name and address. Write to the managing director by name, keeping your letter short and factual and adopting a tone that is more sorrowful than angry. Write clearly and keep a copy. If you want to ensure that the letter will reach the great man himself and will not be opened by his secretary, you could mark the envelope Private and Confidential and sprinkle it with perfume!

  It is a good idea to send a copy of your letter to the managing director of the manufacturer of the product with a brief explanatory note: if he thinks his firm's good name is in jeopardy, he may put pressure on the retailer or settle the problem himself.

Your letter might read:

Dear Mr Helpful,

On April 1st of this year, I bought an Eatwell electric cooker, model number DUD.1, price £299.99, from the Happytown branch of your store. I have the receipt for this purchase.

The automatic timer on the oven did not work at all and I contacted Mr Smiley, the manager at your Happytown store, who advised me to claim under the manufacturer's guarantee. I was willing to do this, but wrote to Mr Smiley on April 5th explaining that if the repair did not solve the problem, I reserved my right to reject the cooker under the Sale of Goods Act.

The Eatwell engineer has called three times – on April 10th, May 6th and May 22nd. On each occasion, the timer was working when the engineer left, but went wrong again within a few weeks.

On June 24th I returned to the store to ask for my money back. To my astonishment, Mr Smiley told me that as the cooker was now nearly three months old he was not prepared to take it back and advised me yet again to contact the manufacturer.

It is clear the cooker is not and never has been 'of merchantable quality' as defined in the Sale of Goods Act 1979 and I am therefore writing to advise you that I am rejecting it and claiming a refund.

I have bought many appliances from your stores and have always found the service pleasant. I am very disappointed at the response I have received so far to my legitimate complaint.

I trust you will be able to put the matter right and look forward to receiving your cheque for £299.99. I hope you will remove the cooker as soon as possible. I am sending a copy of this letter to the managing director of Eatwell Ovens Ltd.

Yours sincerely,
Alec Smart

* If your letter does not bring a satisfactory solution, visit your nearest Citizens' Advice Bureau or Consumer Advice Centre. Sometimes a letter on headed note-paper from an organisation like this brings results when you have drawn a blank. The trading standards or consumer protection department at your local coun-cil offices will also give you useful advice on your case.

* If you paid for the goods on credit and they cost more than £100, the finance company and the seller are equally responsible if they are defective. If the shop refuses to help or has gone out of business, you should write to the finance company explaining the position.

* If you paid by cash or cheque, or you get no joy from the finance company, your next step is to find out whether the retailer belongs to a trade association with a com-plaints procedure. A number of trade associations have drawn up codes of practice approved by the Office of Fair Trading which include a conciliation scheme for complaints. The OFT produces leaflets describing these.

Furniture. The National Association of Retail Furnish-ers and the Scottish House Furnishers' Association will investigate complaints against members and can arrange for an independent examiner to inspect the item in dispute.
Shoes. If you are unhappy with the way a shoe shop belonging to the Footwear Distributors' Federation, the Multiple Shoe Retailers' Federation or the Indepen-dent Footwear Retailers' Association has dealt with your complaint, you can ask for the shoes to be sent to the Footwear Testing Centre for an independent inspection.
Electrical and gas appliances. Any new appliance bought from a member of the Radio, Electrical and Television Retailers' Association (RETRA) is guaran-teed by the shop for 12 months. If a repair under guarantee takes more than 15 days, the shop will either lend you a similar item or extend the guarantee. RETRA has a conciliation service and will investigate com-plaints against members. If you have a complaint about

something bought at an electricity board showroom and you cannot sort the problem out with the shop, contact your area electricity consultative council. Contact your regional gas consumers' council if you have a complaint you cannot resolve about an appliance bought from a gas showroom.

Mail Order. The Mail Order Publishers' Authority, the Mail Order Traders' Association and the Direct Selling Association will investigate complaints made to them in writing against members.

Cars and motorcycles. Four major trade associations involved in car sales, servicing and repairs and four trade associations involved in motorcycle sales and repairs have agreed codes of practice backed by the Office of Fair Trading (see Chapter 9, pages 165, 181).

Do not feel it is pointless to expect help from a trade association that primarily exists to represent its members' interests: some conciliation schemes are genuinely impartial and worth using. However, it must be said that some are not. The only way to find out is to try.

---

* If this does not bring a solution, and you still feel you have a justifiable complaint, you will have to decide whether to take legal action. In Chapter 13, I explain what this involves.

When to Use the Guarantee
When something goes wrong with a product you've bought, your first decision may well be whether to claim under the manufacturer's guarantee. Perhaps the most important thing to remember is that the guarantee is always offered in addition to your legal rights under the Sale of Goods Act and it cannot take these away or affect them in any way.

Sometimes the manufacturer asks you to return a registration card soon after buying the goods. If you do not do this, the manufacturer *could* refuse to honour the guarantee, though he will probably be cooperative if you have proof of the date of purchase.

If you see a clause in a manufacturer's guarantee which implies that the company will not be responsible for any damage caused or loss suffered as a result of their negligence, you can ignore it: such clauses have no effect.

Before you decide whether to claim under a manufacturer's guarantee:

* Read the small print. Find out whether you are expected to pay postage or transport charges. Does the guarantee cover parts and labour? And does it cover the call-out charge for a home visit – to repair large electrical appliances for example? If using the guarantee will cost you money, try approaching the shop first.

* Decide whether you want the goods repaired. Manufacturers usually try to repair products that are under guarantee, and if the fault is a major one it may be difficult to put right. What is more, you will not have the use of the goods while your claim is being processed. If the fault is so serious that you have lost confidence in the product, a repair or replacement will not satisfy you.

* Weigh up whether you want to go back to the shop. If the fault is minor, it may be quicker and easier to contact the manufacturer than to seek compensation from the seller who may be unhelpful. The guarantee can also be useful if the shop has closed down or is difficult for you to get to. If you do have work done under guarantee, tell the shop that you reserve your right to claim under the Sale of Goods Act if the problem is not solved.

Buying at Sale Time

You have exactly the same rights at sale time as you do the rest of the year. Do not let any shopkeeper persuade you otherwise. Of course, if you buy something marked 'seconds', 'imperfect' or 'damaged' you cannot expect it to be in perfect condition. When you see a notice like this, ask what the fault is. You are not expected to know about hidden faults.

Simon Simple bought a spin-drier marked 'shop-soiled' in a sale. He gave it a quick glance and thought it looked fine, but when he got it home he noticed two scratches down one side. He complained to the shop manager who pointed out that the faults were ones he should have noticed.

Alec Smart bought the same model in the same sale. He had noticed the small dent in the lid and it did not bother him. But when he switched the machine on, it made a grinding noise and stopped dead. He returned to the shop and asked for a refund on the grounds that the appliance was not of merchantable quality. The shop agreed.

Buying Secondhand

From a trader
Goods bought from a trader, whether new or second-hand, are covered by the Sale of Goods Act and must be as described, of merchantable quality and fit for their purpose. The definition of 'merchantable quality' depends on the age of the goods and what you paid for them. You would expect a year-old vacuum cleaner bought for £40 to last longer than a five-year-old one bought for £10. But if the £10 one packed up after a week, you would probably be entitled to your money back. The Trade Descriptions Act (see page 54) applies to secondhand goods bought from a trader.

Privately
You have much less protection when you buy privately than you do when you buy from a trader. Goods bought privately do not have to be 'of merchantable quality' or 'fit for their purpose', but they must be 'as described'. So it is wise to ask plenty of questions when you buy

privately and to note down the answers. If you are buying clothes, inspect them thoroughly. Ask to see electrical appliances in operation. If possible take a witness along, especially when you buy an expensive item or one where some technical knowledge would be useful. Another pair of eyes may spot faults you have missed, and if your purchase does not live up to expectations, and you want to take legal action, your witness's evidence may be useful. The Trade Descriptions Act does not apply to private sales.

Because you have so few rights when you buy privately, some rogue dealers in secondhand goods try to pretend that they are private individuals. They may offer to bring the goods to your home so that you cannot see that they have business premises, making some excuse like 'it would be better if you did not come to the house as the wife and I are splitting up.' If you buy something which turns out to be faulty and you suspect that the seller is a dealer masquerading as a private individual, tell the trading standards or consumer protection department at your local council offices.

At an auction
There is little you can do if something you have bought at auction turns out to be faulty. This is because when you buy at auction you are bound by the Conditions of Sale which you will find in the catalogue or on the saleroom walls. These conditions usually take away your rights under the Sale of Goods Act (they can do this because an auction is not classed as a 'consumer sale'), and say things like 'neither the vendor nor the auctioneers are responsible for the authenticity, age, condition or quality of any lot.' If a lot is marked 'WAF' or 'AF' it means 'with all faults' or 'as found' and you can usually take this as a signal that there is something wrong with it.

Auctioneers' catalogues and statements are covered by the Trade Descriptions Act (see page 54). An auctioneer who knowingly described a reproduction desk as 'Georgian' would be committing an offence.

But reputable auctioneers are usually careful about how they describe what they sell and prosecutions are rare.

If the auctioneer makes a statement which turns out to be untrue about a lot you have bought, you may have a case against him for misrepresentation (see page 55), but the courts will expect you to have examined the lots thoroughly before you bid and to have spotted any obvious faults or wrong descriptions. If you do bid at auction:

* Inspect all lots in which you are interested before bidding begins
* Study the catalogue carefully beforehand
* Decide what you are prepared to pay in advance and don't exceed it in the heat of the bidding.

How Goods are Described

When you buy something, you assume that it really is what it is supposed to be. You would not expect a shirt labelled 'pure silk' to be made of polyester, an 'unbreakable' plate to splinter when dropped or a packet of 20 envelopes to contain only 15. The Trade Descriptions Act 1968 protects you against inaccurate descriptions of goods and services. And it is necessary protection, because some traders do try to pull the wool over our eyes in order to increase their profits. In one survey of clothing, trading standards officers found that 28 of the 68 samples tested carried inaccurate fibre content labels. And when *Woman* magazine asked 13 high street butchers for minced beef, it was given a mixture of beef and some other meat in six cases.

The Trade Descriptions Act is part of the criminal law and a trader who breaks it will be prosecuted by a trading standards officer (in Scotland by the Procurator Fiscal). Courts have the power to award compensation to consumers who have suffered as a result of a breach of the Act. If you suspect that something you have bought has been wrongly described in an advertisement, a catalogue, on the packet or on the label or by the trader himself, contact the trading standards or consumer protection department at your local council offices. Even if the court does not award you compensation, a successful prosecution will help any legal action you decide to take against the trader yourself and should protect others from being misled in the same way.

Fibre content

Most woven and knitted articles must carry a label showing what they are made of. If the article is made of more than one fibre, the name and percentage of the main fibre must be given. If the main fibre accounts for less than 85 per cent of the total, the names of the other fibres used must be listed in descending order of weight.

Country of origin

Goods no longer have to carry a label showing where they were made but if they do carry one it must be accurate. If a suit is labelled 'Made in Italy', it must not have been designed, cut and sewn in Taiwan. The problem is that many items consist of parts from several different countries assembled in another. The country where the product takes on its final form is the one that should appear on any label, but no manufacture in the real sense may have taken place there. The best advice is not to pay too much attention to the country of origin marking unless you know what the label really means.

Misrepresentation

If you buy something on the strength of a statement made to you by the seller and that statement turns out to be false, you may be able to sue him for misrepresentation. The Misrepresentation Act 1967 covers new and secondhand goods and property, and sales from traders, private individuals and at auction, so it gives useful protection in cases where the Sale of Goods Act does not apply. The Misrepresentation Act does not apply in Scotland but you have similar rights at common law.

Sales puff and opinions cannot normally be mis-representations.

Alec Smart saw a secondhand leather jacket adver-tised in the local paper. The owner, Mr Sharp, told Alec it looked terrific on him, but when he got it home his wife said it was at least two sizes too big and the colour made him look ill. 'What is more,' she added, 'it's not leather.' Alec could not sue Mr Sharp for misrepresentation over his opinions about the way the jacket looked, but he did have a case against him because he had told him it was leather when it was not.

To prove misrepresentation, you have to establish that an untrue statement of fact was made and this can be hard unless you have a witness or the statement was in writing. You also have to prove that this statement helped persuade you to buy the goods.

There are three kinds of misrepresentation:

- *fraudulent* – when somebody makes a statement know-ing it to be false.

- *negligent* – when a person makes a statement with no reasonable grounds for believing it to be true and it turns out to be false.

- *innocent* – when a person making a statement which turns out to be false has reasonable grounds for think-ing it is true.

What remedy you are entitled to depends partly on the kind of misrepresentation made to you and partly on how quickly you complain. If you act promptly and have not used the goods, you may be able to cancel the contract between you and the seller and get your money

back. If some time has elapsed or you have used the
goods, you may be entitled to compensation.

Misleading Advertisements

If you come across an advertisement which you think is
misleading you should contact:

- the trading standards or consumer protection department at your local council offices – if the advertiser was
  a trader rather than a private individual. He may have
  broken the Trade Descriptions Act (see above, page 54).

- the Advertising Standards Authority – if the advertisement was in printed form. Write to the ASA indicating
  where and when the advert appeared, enclosing a copy
  if possible, and saying what, in your view, is wrong
  with it. The ASA Code of Advertising Practice covers
  virtually every aspect of advertising copy. If the
  Authority suspects that there has been a breach of the
  code, it will investigate and can ask the advertiser to
  withdraw the offending ad. If he refuses, the ASA
  can ask members of the Code of Advertising Practice
  Committee, which includes all the major newspaper
  and magazine publishing organisations, not to publish
  that company's advertising material.

- the Independent Broadcasting Authority – if the advertisement was on television or radio. Write to the IBA
  giving details of the advert, as described in the previous
  paragraph. The Authority will investigate and can ask
  for the advertisement to be withdrawn if it contravenes
  its Code of Advertising Standards and Practice.

If an advertiser still refuses to withdraw a misleading
advert, the Director General of Fair Trading can seek a
court order banning its publication.

If you have bought something on the strength of an
advertisement which turns out to be misleading, you
may be able to obtain compensation.

- If the goods were not 'as described' in the advertisement, you may have a claim under the Sale of Goods Act 1979 (see above, page 40). You would have to prove that the advertisement was intended by the retailer as an offer to contract; the courts might not agree. If a false statement of fact in an advertisement helped persuade you to buy something, you may have a claim for misrepresentation (see above, page 55). This may be easier to prove than breach of contract.

> Alec Smart saw an advertisement in the paper for 'fully washable' armchair covers available by post. He sent away for them, but when they arrived he noticed a label saying 'dry-clean only'. He sent them back because they were not 'as described' and was given a refund: in a case like this there is little doubt the advertisement formed part of the contract. The next day he saw the same ad in the paper, so he contacted the trading standards department at the town hall. They warned the company that they were in breach of the Trade Descriptions Act. The advertisement was withdrawn.

- If the advertiser is found guilty of breaking the Trade Descriptions Act, the court has power to award compensation to consumers who have suffered as a result.

- If the advertiser is found to be in breach of the ASA code, he may offer to compensate you himself.

When You Lose Money

So far in this chapter I have considered what happens when you buy something which turns out to be unsatisfactory. But for thousands of people, the problem is not that they have received faulty goods, but that they have paid money in advance and received nothing at all.

Research by the Office of Fair Trading suggests that each year around 215,000 people lose £18 million between them because they have ordered and paid for goods and services which have not materialised. About a third of these problems relate to orders by post or telephone, and in Chapter 2 I looked at how you can protect yourself when you use mail order (see above, page 36). In Chapter 5 I look at the precautions you can take in another danger zone, home improvements (see below, pages 90–4).

If you are unlucky enough to lose money, either because the trader has done a bunk with your cash or because the company has gone into liquidation, there is very little you can do. A trader who takes money for goods or services which he has no intention of supplying is guilty in England and Wales of obtaining property by deception under the Theft Act 1968 and in Scotland of the common law offence of fraud. The swindler must first be caught, then successfully prosecuted. The courts can make a compensation order when somebody is found guilty under this section of Theft Act. Alternatively, if you have been persuaded to buy something because of a false statement, you may have a civil claim for misrepresentation (see above, page 55). But first you have to nail the culprit.

The Insolvency Act 1985 has improved matters – in theory at least – for people who suffer when a company goes into liquidation. The liquidator can apply to the court to declare a director of an insolvent company personally liable for the company's debts if it can be proved that the director let the company continue trading when he knew or should have known that insolvency was inevitable. This concept is known as wrongful trading. Directors who are found by a court to be unfit to be involved in the management of a company – perhaps because they failed to supply goods or services which had been paid for by consumers – can be disqualified from holding a directorship for a certain time. These provisions are intended to encourage directors whose companies are in financial difficulties to be more aware of their obligations to their customers.

Other provisions in the Act mean that when a company goes into liquidation there should be more money for unsecured creditors such as ordinary consumers.

However, it remains to be seen whether people who have suffered through a company's insolvency are any better off as a result of the Act. Preferential and secured creditors such as the Inland Revenue, Customs and Excise and others will still get the first slice of the disintegrating cake.

For these reasons, you should be very wary of paying money 'up-front'. Unless the amount is so small that you would not miss it, or the company so well-established that its disappearance would be unthinkable (there are very few which fall into that category), you should protect yourself by following the buy-laws:

☞ If the goods or services cost more than £100, pay by credit (see Chapter 11, pages 221–3).

☞ If you are paying in advance for home improvements, choose a company belonging to one of the trade associations which operate a scheme to protect consumer pre-payments (see Chapter 5, page 94).

☞ If you are buying by mail order from a newspaper or magazine advertisement, make sure you are covered by one of the Mail Order Protection Schemes (see Chapter 2, page 34).

☞ If you are booking a package holiday choose a tour operator who is a member of the Association of British Travel Agents (see Chapter 8, page 152).

4

Safety

We tend to take the safety of what we buy for granted. We assume we won't get an electric shock from our new iron, a skin rash from our cosmetics or a serious injury from a toy gun.

In fact, although the vast majority of goods on sale are perfectly safe, hundreds of potentially dangerous items have reached the shops, mainly from abroad. Hair-curling brushes which could have electrocuted the user, make-up kits containing dangerous levels of lead and a toy dart which nearly blinded a small boy are just three of the many unsafe products that have been bought in recent years.

However, the passing of the Consumer Safety (Amendment) Act 1986 should lead to a decrease in the number of unsafe goods in our shops. Further changes in the law are expected over the next year or so, which will impose on traders a general duty to make sure the goods they supply are safe. These should also greatly improve matters.

The Law on Safety
Safety legislation works in various ways.

Regulations made under the Consumer Protection Acts 1961 and 1971 and the Consumer Safety Act 1978 make it illegal to sell certain types of goods unless they conform to statutory safety standards. There are more than 30 different regulations covering a wide range of products from babies' dummies to cars. They apply to almost all goods sold by traders – new or secondhand – but not to private sales. Among the products covered are:

- prams and pushchairs – including their brakes, their stability and their locking devices
- children's nightdresses and dressing gowns – must not be of highly flammable material
- upholstered furniture – must not ignite when in contact with a smouldering cigarette and must carry a label stating how it would burn if exposed to a lighted match. Furniture with a green label has passed the match test and that with a red label might fail
- children's upholstered furniture – must pass a flammability test
- toys – materials should be non-toxic and not highly flammable; there should be no sharp points or spikes; parts such as eyes on soft toys should be secure
- electrical appliances – including their earthing and insulation and general electrical safety
- crash helmets – their strength
- cosmetics – must be safe in normal use
- cars – including seat belts, safety glass, reflectors and lights
- paraffin heaters – must be stable and must cut out within 15 seconds if tipped over; they must not give out smoke or excessive carbon monoxide
- medicines – aspirin and paracetamol must be sold in sealed dosage units such as blister packs or in child-resistant containers
- household chemicals – from 1988 hazardous products such as white spirits, oven and drain cleaner, paint stripper, strong bleach and disinfectant must be sold in child-resistant containers.

Although these regulations cover many products, they also leave many gaps. There are regulations covering children's pushchairs, for example, but none on cots, highchairs and babywalkers. Paint on children's toys must not contain high lead levels, but there are no controls on the lead in children's painted furniture. The trader who sold the plastic dart that nearly blinded a child was not breaking the law because the toy safety regulations do not cover this kind of product. A costume doll whose head was secured with a spike has been ruled by some courts to be a 'novelty' rather than a toy and therefore not covered by toy safety regulations. However, these loopholes should be closed if and when the general duty to trade safely becomes law.

There are various steps which the government and local authorities can take to deal with unsafe products:

A notice to warn served on a trader obliges him to publish a warning about goods he has sold.

A prohibition notice is a stronger weapon which prevents the trader concerned from selling specific goods considered to be unsafe.

A prohibition order bans the sale of specific goods by *any* trader for up to 12 months. In time, prohibition orders are often replaced by regulations which have to be approved by Parliament.

A suspension notice enables trading standards officers to order a trader to stop selling goods which they suspect are breaking safety requirements. It runs for six months, and in the meantime a decision must be made on whether to bring a prosecution. Alternatively, officers can seize the goods for the same length of time.

To prevent unsafe imported products reaching the shops, customs officers can alert trading standards officers when they come across goods in certain 'problem categories'. If these are thought to be dangerous, trading standards officers can seize them. They can also test samples taken from importers or manufacturers to make sure these comply with safety legislation.

Alec Smart bought an electric frying pan from Mr
Shady, a market trader. When he looked at it closely
at home he was alarmed to see live parts were
clearly visible. He took it back to the trader who
said there was nothing wrong with it. So Alec took
the frying pan to the trading standards department
at his local council offices. They agreed that it
looked dangerous and issued a suspension notice,
banning Mr Shady from selling it. After having the
pan tested by experts, who confirmed that it was
potentially dangerous, the trading standards
department successfully prosecuted Mr Shady for
a breach of the Electrical Equipment (Safety)
Regulations. Following this, Alec took legal action
against the trader under the Sale of Goods Act
because the pan was not of merchantable quality.
After receiving the summons, Mr Shady refunded
Alec the cost of the pan.

How to Avoid Unsafe Products

Do not take safety for granted when you shop. Before
you make your decision, think about the safety features.
Take toys out of their boxes and examine them – sometimes you as a parent can spot potential hazards a
manufacturer has missed. With gas and electrical
appliances, ask for a demonstration in the shop where
possible, so you can gain an idea of what they are like to
use.

You cannot always tell whether a product is safe
merely by looking at it. In general, you give yourself
more protection by buying a well-known brand or from
a big-name store because reputable manufacturers and
retailers operate stringent quality control checks and
do not want to risk their good name by selling dangerous goods. Buying from a here-today-gone-tomorrow
street trader is riskier. However, even the best companies can make mistakes: for a time a well-known
chain store sold a child's bed with paint containing

dangerously high levels of lead. As soon as this was pointed out, the bed was withdrawn from sale.

Some products carry symbols showing that they have been made to certain standards. Although not all of these standards relate to safety, the symbols can be useful in helping you to choose well-made products.

British Standards

British Standards are technical specifications for a vast range of different goods, drawn up by committees of the British Standards Institution (BSI). These committees are made up of people with an interest in and knowledge of particular products and may include manufacturers, retailers, and representatives of professional bodies and consumer organisations.

There are about 9,500 British Standards, of which about 350 apply to consumer goods. Compliance with most of them is entirely voluntary. The only compulsory standards are those that form the basis of safety regulations. If you see the letters BS on a product, followed by a number, it means that the manufacturer is claiming his product complies with the standard and he can be prosecuted if it does not. But the number alone does not mean that the product has been independently tested.

THE KITEMARK

BS 857

This means that samples of the product have been tested by the British Standards Institution and comply with the relevant standard. Not all standards are concerned with safety; many relate to the quality of the product and its performance in use. But you can be fairly confident that a product bearing the Kitemark is unlikely to be dangerous. If you want to check exactly what the standard for a particular product means, you will find a complete set of British Standards in the reference section of most central public libraries.

THE SAFETY MARK

Products which carry this sign conform to British Standards concerned with safety only and samples have been tested by BSI inspectors.

THE BEAB MARK

For electric blankets only   BEAB-Mark of Safety

These are found on electrical appliances and mean that the product has been tested by and approved to the relevant British Standard by the British Electrotechnical Approvals Board and found to be safe.

The Design Centre label

Contrary to popular belief, a product carrying this label does not simply have to *look* nice. It must be well-made, easy to use, suitable for its purpose, simple to maintain

and value for money and must comply with the relevant British safety standards.

If You Buy an Unsafe Product

If you buy a product which you suspect is unsafe, take it back to the trader who sold it to you. A dangerous product is not of 'merchantable quality' as defined in the Sale of Goods Act and you are entitled to reject it and ask for your money back (see Chapter 3, page 42). You should tell the trading standards or consumer protection department at your local council offices so that they can investigate.

If something you have bought injures you or damages your property because it is defective and unsafe, you may be able to sue the supplier:

● for breach of contract under the Sale of Goods Act; in this case your claim would be against the shopkeeper.

● for 'breach of statutory duty'; you can only do this if the supplier is found guilty of breaking regulations made under the Consumer Protection and Consumer Safety Acts.

● for negligence (see below).

In some cases it is more appropriate to sue the manufacturer or importer than the shopkeeper. For example:

* when somebody else is injured as a result of a defect in a product you have bought. If you bought a hairdrier which shot out flames, injuring your daughter, she would not be able to sue under the Sale of Goods Act because there was no contract between her and the seller of the goods.

* if the shop has closed down.

* if you were claiming larger damages than you thought the shopkeeper could meet.

Negligence

Manufacturers have a duty to consumers to take reasonable care that the products they market are safe. To prove that a manufacturer has been negligent, you have to establish that:

- you have been injured or your property damaged as a result of a defect in the product
- the injuries or damage were the result of the trader's failure to take reasonable care
- the trader owes a duty of care to you, the injured person.

Before you contemplate bringing a negligence claim, you should take legal advice: negligence is likely to be denied and can be difficult to prove. Taking a case to court can be very expensive.

Product Liability

From 1988 suing a supplier whose product has caused you injury should be easier. By then, at the insistence of the EEC, Britain will have introduced product liability legislation. This means manufacturers and importers will be responsible for injury or damage caused by a defective product that they have put into circulation *regardless of whether they were negligent (at fault) or not.* This concept is known as 'no fault' liability.

Under the new legislation it will be enough for you to prove that the injury or damage was caused by a defect in the product: you will not have to prove that the company concerned was at fault in failing to take reasonable care. A defective product is one that does not provide the standard of safety a person is entitled to expect, bearing in mind factors like its intended use and when it was marketed.

However, it seems likely that a producer will not be liable if he can prove that no producer of his type of product could possibly have discovered the defect, taking into account the state of scientific and technical knowledge at the time when he put the product into circulation.

Manufacturers have pressed for this 'development risks' defence, arguing that without it they would be frightened to make innovations in their products. The government believes that it will be so difficult for manufacturers to plead the defence successfully that they will not be able to shelter behind it easily. But there is a fear that its very existence will deter consumers from bringing a case and will make nonsense of the idea of 'no fault' liability.

Product liability legislation will be aimed at manufacturers and importers. But where these cannot be identified, you will be able to sue the supplier furthest up the distribution chain. You will have to sue within three years of discovering the damage, the defect and the identity of the producer, and you will not be able to sue once the product has been on the market for ten years or more.

5

Services

So far we have looked mainly at what happens when we buy goods such as a three-piece suite, a shirt or a pound of tomatoes. Just as often, though, our money is spent on services – work carried out by one person for another. The range of services we use in everyday life is enormous: doctors, dentists, gas and electricity boards, hotels, hairdressers, solicitors, shoemenders, banks, builders, carpenters and car mechanics.

Unfortunately, services are just as likely to cause us problems as the goods we buy. Research carried out by the Office of Fair Trading suggests that as many as 13.5 million people may be unhappy about services they have paid for in any 12-month period. Nearly a quarter of the complaints in the OFT survey related to building work and a fifth to public utilities and transport. Car repairs and professional services also came quite high on the list. Sadly the OFT also found that people who complained about poor service were not likely to get much joy – at least the first time round. Fewer than half the problems were sorted out on the first complaint.

Don't be depressed by these dismal statistics. If you choose with care who you use, take a few precautions before you commit yourself and know how to complain when things go wrong, you stand a better chance of coming out on top.

A whole range of legislation protects you when you visit the hairdressers or call in the plumber, just as the law protects you when you buy a new fridge or a toy for your child. Perhaps the most important piece of legislation in this area is the Supply of Goods and Services Act 1982. This states that, unless both parties have agreed otherwise, any service must be performed:

- with reasonable care and skill
- within a reasonable time
- at a reasonable cost.

The Act applies to virtually all services carried out in the course of a business where there is a contract between the two parties. The contract need not be in writing. When somebody offers to provide a service for a fee and you accept the offer, a contract is made. If the person with whom you have made the contract uses a sub-contractor, the original contractor is responsible for his work, too.

The Act does not apply in Scotland but you have similar rights at common law.

The Standard of the Work and Materials

There are two kinds of service. In one category are those contractors who supply some parts or materials when carrying out their work: builders, car mechanics and electricians are in this group. Your contract with them is for **work and materials.** In the other category are those contractors who perform a service that leaves you with nothing more than you originally owned: dry cleaners, furniture removers and solicitors are in this group.

The Supply of Goods and Services Act says that any materials supplied as part of a contract for work and materials must be *as described, of merchantable quality* and *fit for their purpose*. In other words, you have the same rights as you would had you bought the materials yourself. If they are faulty, do not do the job properly or are not as the trader described them, then you have a claim against him. However, if you insisted that he use certain materials he will not be liable if they turn out to be the wrong ones for the job.

Simon Simple called in a plumber to supply and instal a new hot water cylinder. The plumber advised him that as there were two adults and three teenagers in the house he should have a 'Supasize'. Simon was rather shocked at the price and decided to opt for a 'Mini' instead. When Simon had to face the family fury because the tank would provide only two baths in an evening, he complained to the plumber that the cylinder was not fit for its purpose. The plumber reminded him of the advice he had given and pointed out – correctly – that Simon did not have a case. However, a few days later and entirely by coincidence, the cylinder started leaking. The plumber accepted that it was not of merchantable quality and, after Simon had paid the extra, installed a Supasize version.

Any service must be performed with reasonable care and skill – this means the level of skill you would expect of an ordinary trader doing that kind of work. So if your suit comes out of the dry cleaners three shades lighter than it went in, or a treatment at the hairdressers leaves you scalped, or your new home extension resembles the leaning tower of Pisa, you will have a case against the contractor if you can prove that he did not exercise reasonable care and skill in carrying out the work.

When things go wrong

* If, after being given ample opportunity, a contractor fails to carry out a piece of work satisfactorily, find out from other traders what it would cost to put the matter right and deduct this amount from the bill when you pay the original contractor.

* If – as is quite likely – you do not notice the poor workmanship until after you have paid the bill, you are in a weaker position. Supposing you take your television to a repairer because the picture has narrowed to

half the size of the screen. The shop assures you it has fixed the fault, but when you get the TV home you find the picture is as bad as before. Give the shop a chance to put things right. If they fail, take the set to another repairer. If he says it cannot be repaired, it may be that the original shop did exercise reasonable care and skill and you will have to let the matter rest there. If, however, he rectifies the problem, sue the first trader for the cost of the successful repair.

* If you have not paid but the trader has your goods – a camera you took in for repair, say – your position is even weaker. Pay for the service, but write 'paid under protest' across the bill. Then consider starting legal action to get your money back (see Chapter 13).

* Sometimes the problem simply cannot be put right. If the dry cleaners lose your suit, the chemist exposes the film of your once-in-a-lifetime trip to the North Pole or the surveyor fails to notice that your new house is riddled with dry rot, then the damage cannot be undone. In cases like this, you are entitled to compensation – for the value of the suit, for example, the distress caused by the loss of the precious film and the cost of eliminating the dry rot – if you can prove that the contractor did not take reasonable care.

* If a contractor injures you or loses or damages your property as a result of not taking reasonable care, you may be able to sue him for negligence. This would apply even if you did not employ him yourself – in which case you would not have a case against him under the Supply of Goods and Services Act.

The Time the Job Takes

If you want a service performed within a certain time, make this clear at the outset, preferably in writing. If possible, have it written on the order sheet or in the contract that you want your daughter's wedding dress altered by the big day or the nursery decorated before the baby is due.

If you do not agree a completion date, the contractor must finish the job within a reasonable time. You can find out what this is by asking a few other traders how long they would take.

When things go wrong

* If you have agreed a firm date and the work is not completed on time, the contract has been broken and you can claim compensation. In practice, it is generally wiser first to make *time of the essence of the contract* as described in the next paragraph.

* If you have not agreed a completion date, and you think the contractor is taking longer than is reasonable over the job, write to him setting a date by which the work must be finished and explaining that if it is not completed by then you will cancel the contract and may claim damages. You must give the contractor a reasonable time to complete the job bearing in mind the work involved. This is called making *time of the essence of the contract*. If the work is not finished by the specified date, you are entitled to cancel the contract, call in another contractor to finish the job and sue the first contractor for the cost of completing the work plus compensation for any inconvenience caused. Obviously you should think carefully before taking this step.

* If the contractor has your goods – a watch in for repair, perhaps, or a car for bodywork – you are in a more difficult position. Again, the first step is to make time of the essence of the contract. If this does not achieve results, threaten legal action for breach of contract in order to recover your belongings. You could also threaten to buy or hire a replacement item and to charge this to the original contractor.

* If a company claims in its sales literature or advertisements that it will carry out a service within a certain time – 24-hour film processing, say, or 48-hour curtain cleaning – then it is committing an offence under the

Trade Descriptions Act 1968 if it fails to live up to its slogan. Tell your local trading standards or consumer protection department. If the firm is found guilty, the court has power to award compensation to consumers who have suffered. Even if you do not obtain compensation this way, a successful prosecution should lend weight to any claim you have against the company.

What it Costs

Agreeing a price – estimates and quotations
Whenever possible, find out how much a job is going to cost *before* you agree to have it done.

A contractor may give you a rough price or a firm one. In law a rough price, called an **estimate,** is not legally binding. A firm one, called a **quotation,** is. The trouble is that traders and consumers often use the word estimate when they actually mean a quotation. If you want a firm price for a piece of work, say so and wherever possible get the contractor to put the quotation in writing. A quotation should state what work is being done and what the charge will be.

Simon Simple called in a roofer to fix some loose tiles. The man gave the roof a quick glance and told Simon the work would cost 'about £75'. When he descended from his ladder two hours later, he informed Simon that the job was more tricky than he thought and the bill would be £100. He was entitled to do this because he had not given a firm quotation. Simon was cross, but he still thought the cost was reasonable so he paid up. If the bill had been excessive, he need only have paid what was reasonable (see below, page 76).

Alec Smart called in the same roofer and insisted that the man give him a firm quotation, in writing, for the job. Once again, the roofer underestimated the amount of work involved, but this time he was bound by the price he had quoted. If the roofer had overestimated the work and finished the job in much less time than he had planned, Alec would still have had to pay the agreed price.

Extra work

It is a good idea to agree in advance what work you want done. You do not have to pay for work that you did not ask for. If Simon's roofer had informed him that he had noticed his guttering was cracked and had fixed that too, for an extra £25, Simon would not have had to pay as he had not asked him to do the job. If however, Simon had said 'if you find any other problems while you are up there, fix them for me', that would have given the roofer a free hand to do whatever work was necessary and to make a reasonable charge.

If something needs repair and you have no idea what the fault is or how much it will cost to fix, ask the contractor to investigate and then give you a quotation for the job. Alternatively tell him the maximum you are prepared to pay for the repair; otherwise – especially in the case of relatively inexpensive items such as small electrical goods or cheap watches – you could easily end up spending more on the repair than the goods are worth. Some firms that do repairs make a charge for a quotation, which they may deduct from the final bill if you decide to have the work done. Check in advance whether the quotation is free.

When things go wrong

Unless you have agreed a firm price in advance, the contractor can only charge what is reasonable for the work he has done. You can find out what is reasonable by asking other traders in the area.

If you are presented with a bill you think is exorbitant, do not pay it. Find out what a reasonable charge for the work would be and pay that, making it clear how you have arrived at the figure and stating that your payment is in full and final settlement of the bill. If the contractor thinks he has been underpaid, he may try to sue you for the rest of his bill. If he knows that his first invoice was excessive, he may settle for what you have offered. Alternatively, you could pay the contractor what you think is a reasonable sum on the spot and leave him to sue you for the rest if he chooses.

Life becomes more complicated when payment is being demanded by a 6-foot plumber with both feet firmly planted on your living room carpet and a menacing look in his eye or when the repairer who has just presented you with a £25 bill for mending your toaster will not relinquish the machine until you pay up. In a case like this, make it plain that you think the bill is unreasonable by writing 'paid under protest' across the invoice. Keep a copy of the bill yourself. Find out what a reasonable charge for the work would be and sue the contractor for the amount you have overpaid. If you do not protest about an inflated bill immediately, the court may take the view – if you subsequently sue – that as you did not complain at the time you accepted the amount as reasonable.

Other Problems

Exclusion clauses

Generally speaking, once you have made a contract, it is binding on both parties, whatever it says. However, this is not always true if the contractor has tried to limit your legal rights in some way. In the past, contractors could – and often did – cram their contracts with exclusion clauses, usually set out in minute print on the back of the document. In a famous case shortly before the law was changed, the widow of a man who drowned in a murky holiday camp pool was not awarded any compensation for his death – even though the judge acknowledged that it was partly due to the camp's negligence in not maintaining the pool properly – because an exclusion clause in the booking conditions limited the company's liability for death or injury 'however caused'.

Today, thanks to the Unfair Contract Terms Act 1977, the picture is very different. Certain exclusion clauses are completely invalid in law and others are invalid unless the trader can prove they are fair and reasonable in the circumstances. The Act applies to written and verbal contracts, booking conditions and notices displayed in shops. The Act says that contractors cannot:

- limit their responsibility for death or injury caused by their negligence
- exclude or limit your rights under the Sale of Goods Act 1979. This means that whenever goods are supplied to you by a trader they must be *as described, of merchantable quality* and *fit for their purpose.*

The Act says that traders cannot rely on the following exclusion clauses unless they are reasonable:

- clauses which attempt to limit the trader's responsibility for loss or damage caused by his negligence. Notices which say 'All articles left at the owner's risk' or 'No responsibility is accepted for loss or damage however caused' fall into this category. In some circumstances a notice like this might be considered reasonable; in others, not.

> Simon Simple hung up his coat in a restaurant. Near the pegs was a prominent sign saying 'We accept no responsibility for the loss of articles left here'. During the evening the coat was stolen. Simon took the restaurant to court, claiming that they had been negligent in not taking reasonable care of his belongings. But the judge decided that the notice was a reasonable one in the circumstances.
>
> Alec Smart handed his coat into a dry cleaners displaying a similar notice. When he came to collect it, the owner told him it had been 'mislaid' and refused to compensate him, pointing to the notice disclaiming responsibility. Alec took the shop to court. In his case the judge decided that the owner

> had indeed been negligent and that his attempt to
> deny responsibility was unreasonable.

- Clauses which attempt to allow the trader to break the contract or to do something substantially different from what you would have expected from the contract. A clause in a holiday brochure which said that the tour operator could alter any aspect of the holiday at will without paying you compensation for the inconvenience would fall into this category.

- clauses which attempt to limit a contractor's responsibility for misrepresentation (see below). Scottish consumers do not have this particular protection.

Misrepresentation
If a contractor makes a statement which turns out to be false, you may be able to sue him for misrepresentation (see Chapter 3, page 55). If, for example, a double glazing salesman assured you that his product would cut your heating bills by 20 per cent, you might have a case against his company if he turned out to be wrong – particularly if he had put this promise in writing. If the double glazing company pointed to a clause in their contract disclaiming responsibility for any statements made by their sales force, they would have to prove that such a clause was reasonable.

How to Complain about Services

* If you have a complaint, try to sort it out with the trader concerned. If contacting him by telephone or in person does not bring a solution, write to him, setting out clearly and concisely, with dates, what service he was to have performed and what has gone wrong. Keep copies of all your correspondence and, if possible, take photographs of the problem. If this does not bring a satisfactory response, write to the consumer services

department or the managing director at the company's head office.

* If you have paid by credit for a service costing more than £100 the finance company and the contractor are equally responsible if things go wrong. So if you are getting nowhere with the contractor or he has gone out of business, contact the finance company and explain the position to them (see Chapter 11, pages 221–3).

* If you are still not satisfied, contact your nearest Citizen's Advice Bureau, Consumer Advice Centre or the trading standards or consumer protection department at your local council offices. They may take up the matter on your behalf.

* If the firm belongs to a trade association, find out if there is a conciliation procedure for disputes between its members and their customers.

* If you still have no success, you will have to decide whether to take legal action (see Chapter 13).

Codes of Practice

When choosing a contractor, you will give yourself extra protection by going to a firm which belongs to one of the trade associations that have a code of practice backed by the Office of Fair Trading. It must be said that while some codes seem to be working well – with firms bound by them attracting fewer complaints than firms which are not – other codes have made little difference to standards in the industry concerned. As a general rule, though, you are likely to have less cause for complaint if you use a code member. The OFT produces useful leaflets describing each of these codes.

DRY CLEANING AND LAUNDRY

Members of the Association of British Laundry, Cleaning and Rental Services – more than 75 per cent of the launderers and dry cleaners (but not launderettes) in the country – have agreed not to limit their responsibility for negligence, so you should not see notices in their shops saying things like 'compensation limited to £50 per item'. The association operates a customer advisory service which will help resolve disputes. It can arrange for articles to be tested at an independent research centre.

SHOE REPAIRS

Members of the National Association of Multiple Shoe Repairers and the Society of Master Shoe Repairers undertake to display a current list of prices showing the main services they offer and the materials used. They will take responsibility for unsatisfactory repairs and put them right without charge. They can also arrange for a free test report on a repair which is the cause of complaint.

FUNERALS

Members of the National Association of Funeral Directors will supply a price list to clients and give a written estimate which they will not exceed without permission. They will arrange a simple basic funeral if requested. The association operates a conciliation service to help resolve disputes between its members and their clients.

GLASS AND DOUBLE GLAZING

Members of the Glass and Glazing Federation, which represents the major double glazing companies, will give consumers who have signed a contract away from business premises – for example at home – a firm quotation in writing and a five-day cooling-off period in which they may change their minds. If a survey reveals that the company has underestimated the amount of work involved, it will give you the option of accepting the new price or cancelling the contract. Member companies must give you a delivery date. If the installation cannot be completed by then, they must explain how you can make *time of the essence* of the contract (see above, page 74). The GGF will try to settle disputes between members and their customers and can arrange for an independent expert to inspect a double glazing installation which causes complaint.

PHOTOGRAPHIC SERVICES

Members of the seven main trade associations in the photographic industry adhere to the Photocode. Shops which carry out film processing will clearly display prices for developing and printing. If a Photocode member advertises a free film offer, he must make the full cost of processing clear. If you use a professional photographer who belongs to the British Institute of Professional Photography or the Master Photographers' Association, he will tell you his fees and business terms at the outset and give you a delivery date which he will do his best to keep. If you have a piece of equipment repaired by a Photocode member, he will give you a receipt listing the work to be done and the estimated cost, if known. If more work is involved than first thought, you will be asked if you want the repair to be done. Most repairs will be completed within 21 days. Repairs will be guaranteed.

CARS AND MOTORCYCLES

Four major trade associations involved in car sales, servicing and repairs and four involved in motorcycle sales and repairs have agreed codes of practice backed by the OFT (see Chapter 9, pages 165, 181–3).

PACKAGE HOLIDAYS

Ninety per cent of travel agents and tour operators belong to the Association of British Travel Agents, which has drawn up a code of practice backed by the OFT (see Chapter 8, pages 150–1).

ELECTRICAL APPLIANCE SERVICING

The Association of Manufacturers of Domestic Electrical Appliances, the Radio, Electrical and Television Retailers' Association and the area electricity boards operate codes of practice backed by the OFT covering the sale, repair and servicing of electrical appliances (see below, pages 85–6).

Choosing a Contractor

On the following pages and in later chapters I shall look in more detail at a wide range of different services and suggest steps you can take to protect yourself against problems. To summarise what I have said so far, here are the buy-laws to follow when choosing a contractor to perform any kind of service:

☞ Always choose the firm or individual you use with care. If possible go by personal recommendation. If the firm belongs to a trade association which has a code of practice backed by the Office of Fair Trading, so much the better.

☞ Make it clear to the contractor what you want him to do and what he should do if more work is involved than he first thought.

☞ Whenever possible get a firm price for the job in writing in advance. If this is not possible, set a maximum price you are prepared to pay and ask to be contacted if the final bill is likely to be higher than this.

☞ If you want the job done within a certain time, make this clear in writing at the outset.

Call-Outs: Household Repairs and Emergencies

Domestic appliances: how to avoid a call-out
It can cost £20 or more just to get a contractor to your front door and then you may be told that your appliance is not worth repairing or, equally infuriating, that the problem is so slight you could have fixed it yourself had you known the cause. Any repairman will tell you that many of his calls are totally unnecessary – caused by the owner's failure to read the operating instructions properly! Before you reach for the telephone, check that:

* the controls are properly set – if there are small children in the house, they may have tampered with the machine without your knowing.

* the mains socket is working – plug in another appliance to the same socket.

* the fuse in the plug has not blown – replace it with another of the same value; fuses age and can blow for no reason.

* the flex is correctly wired to the plug and that all the screws are secure.

* the inlet hose on washing machines and dishwashers is not kinked.

* the aerial lead on televisions is plugged in at both ends.

* Finally, switch the appliance on and off quickly twice only. If it is a minor fault it may clear itself.

If you need a service call
When you summon a repairman:

* Ask on the telephone what the minimum charge will be. If you think it is too steep, shop around – but beware of cowboy repairers who do not know what they are doing. You are less likely to come unstuck if you use the manufacturer's own engineers, those authorised by the manufacturer to service their appliances or members of a reputable trade association.

* Give the make of the appliance, the model and serial numbers and the nature of the fault. If you think you know what the problem is, or what spare part is likely to be needed, say so. If you are very lucky, the engineer may actually bring it with him!

* Give your name, address and a daytime phone number.

* If possible give the engineer a few alternative times when it will be suitable to call.

* Say whether or not the appliance is under guarantee.

☞ **Remember!**
If you provide the engineer with a cup of tea you could find yourself paying for the time he takes to drink it. This has happened.

═══════════════════════════════════════

Codes of practice
The three major organisations representing retailers and manufacturers of electrical goods have drawn up codes of practice backed by the Office of Fair Trading covering the sale, repair and servicing of electrical appliances. As with all codes, some companies stick to them more diligently than others. If you think you are getting poor service, draw the company's attention to what the code says.

THE AMDEA AND ELECTRICITY BOARD CODES
The Association of Manufacturers of Domestic Electrical Appliances represents most British manufacturers of what are called 'white goods' – that is, appliances like washing machines, fridges and electric cookers which are normally found in the kitchen, and water and storage heaters. The area electricity boards sell and service electrical appliances. Their codes say that:

● Whenever possible, a first visit should be made within three working days of your phonecall. Eighty per cent of repair jobs should be completed on the first visit. If a second visit is necessary, it should be made within 15 working days of the first. Where this is not possible, you should be told
● You should be offered an appointment on a particular day and preferably told whether it will be in the morning or the afternoon. When the engineer cannot keep his appointment you should, if possible, be told
● When you phone you should be told of any minimum charges
● Whenever possible you should be given a rough estimate of the cost of the repair and a written estimate if you ask for one

- Labour and spare parts will be guaranteed
- Essential spare parts will be available for between five and 15 years – depending on the type of appliance – after the model has been discontinued.

AMDEA will act as a mediator in disputes between its members and their customers. If you have a complaint about an area electricity board, your area consultative council will investigate (see Chapter 7, pages 128–9).

THE RETRA CODE
The Radio, Electrical and Television Retailers' Association represents more than 4,000 shops selling white goods and brown goods – televisions, radios and hi-fi equipment. The provisions of the RETRA code are similar to those in the AMDEA and electricity board codes. RETRA operates a conciliation service for disputes between retailers and their customers.

Maintenance contracts and extended warranties – who needs them?

MAINTENANCE CONTRACTS
Maintenance contracts offer 'peace of mind' – for a fee. You pay a certain amount each year: the price depends on how reliable the type of appliance is and how expensive to repair: washing machines come pricey, vacuum cleaners much cheaper. As a contract holder you can normally call in the service engineer as often as you like without charge. The contract usually covers parts and labour for any repairs, including those caused by the ageing of the appliance, and may include an annual service. The Consumers' Association has consistently said that maintenance contracts seem poor value for money and believes you are generally better off paying for repairs as they occur. If each year you put the money a maintenance contract would have cost into a building society, you would almost certainly amass enough to cover your repair bills over the first five year's of the appliance's life. Only the unfortunate

owners of a rogue machine would spend more. And if you were lucky enough not to touch the money it would be there to put towards a new machine when yours gave up the ghost.

EXTENDED WARRANTIES

These work differently from maintenance contracts. You pay once, normally soon after purchase, and the warranty usually extends the terms of the manufacturer's guarantee for a further four years. The cost is generally lower than for maintenance contracts, but the cover may well be less comprehensive. Warranties are offered by manufacturers, retailers and specialist companies. If you are considering taking one out, read the terms carefully. In particular find out:

* whether the warranty covers wear and tear through normal use – some do not.

* whether the repair is carried out free of charge – in some schemes you have to pay and are reimbursed later; if this is the case, find out how long you will have to wait for your money.

* whether the warranty is transferable if you sell the appliance.

* whether there are any other exclusions such as damage by misuse or damage to the outside casing of the appliance.

You should also find out who is actually providing the warranty. If it is the manufacturer, your money is safe – unless of course the company goes out of business. But if it is offered by a trader or outside agency, it should be underwritten by an authorised insurance company. Find out which one and contact the Department of Trade and Industry's Insurance Division to make sure the company is authorised to handle extended warranty business. In one notorious case, customers buying at major chain stores were offered an extended warranty backed by an insurance company which was not authorised to handle that kind of business. When the company was wound up, many people were left with worthless pieces of paper. If the warranty is not insurance-based, beware.

Other repairs and emergencies

The field of household repairs is one where the cowboy workman can flourish. You may well be desperate when you call him – with water cascading from a burst pipe or no central heating and temperatures at $-5°C$ – and he knows it. He may take advantage of this by presenting you with an outrageous bill or, worse, by leaving you with an inadequate or even dangerous repair. A builder who fitted a water tap to a gas pipe and an 'electrician' who connected up an entire house with flimsy bell wire are just two – true – horror stories. When you call in a plumber, electrician or other contractor to your home, follow the 'buy-laws':

☞ Keep a list of reliable workmen handy. Try them out on non-emergency jobs first and they will be more likely to respond when a crisis occurs. What you want to avoid is having to pick a firm out of the Yellow Pages with a pin in an emergency.

☞ If you do need to find a contractor quickly, go for one who belongs to a trade association or other organisation which monitors its members' standards of work (see below).

☞ Learn to cope with the worst emergencies so that you won't be driven into the arms of a cowboy out of sheer desperation (see below).

☞ Whenever possible, agree a price for the job beforehand (see above, page 75).

PLUMBING

Find out how to turn off the water supply in an emergency. Make sure all the family know where the main stopcock is and can turn it on and off easily. If you have a burst pipe, shut the water off, drain the cold water system but leave the hot taps alone and switch off the central heating and the immersion heater. Water authorities operate a 24-hour emergency service and will cut off the supply to your home until you can find a plumber. Look under 'Water' in the telephone directory.

The Institute of Plumbing keeps an eye on the standards of its members' work. Write to the Institute enclosing a stamped addressed envelope for a list of registered plumbers. Most water authorities can also supply the names of plumbers; it will not vouch for them, but they are unlikely to be rogues.

ELECTRICS

If you suddenly find yourself in the dark, check fuses first, remembering to switch off the mains supply to the house beforehand. Keep the cupboard containing the fuse box free from clutter and store a torch nearby. All electricity boards operate a 24-hour emergency service but – depending on where the fault lies – you may have to pay. Look under 'Electricity' in the telephone directory.

Choose an electrician who is on the register of the National Inspection Council for Electrical Installation Contracting. He has passed an examination and his work is regularly checked. Electricity showrooms and Citizens' Advice Bureaux have copies of the register, or you can write to the NICEIC. Firms belonging to the Electrical Contractors' Association have been vetted. The association guarantees its members' installations against bad workmanship and will arrange for a job to be completed at no extra cost if the member who started it goes out of business.

GAS

If you smell gas, stub out cigarettes and don't use electrical switches. Open windows and doors and do a quick check to see if a pilot light has blown out. If not, turn off the supply at the main gas tap – usually near the meter – and call the gas board. Look under 'Gas' in the telephone directory. Emergency visits are free provided they take less than 30 minutes or require only inexpensive parts. In other cases, whether you pay depends on where the leak is.

For repairs or gas installations, call a British Gas installer or one who is registered with the Confederation for the Registration of Gas Installers. CORGI installers have their work regularly checked. Copies of the register are kept at British Gas showrooms and Citizens' Advice Bureaux. An installer who does not follow the Gas Safety Regulations may be committing a criminal offence. There are plans for all competent gas fitters to be issued with a certificate which householders will be able to ask to see.

CENTRAL HEATING

If you have gas central heating call a British Gas installer or one who is registered with CORGI (see previous paragraph). If you have electric heating choose somebody on the NICEIC register, preferably a member of the ECA (see above). The Heating and Ventilating Contractors' Association monitor their members' work and offer a guarantee against faulty workmanship and materials.

Home Improvements

It is a sad fact that if you have work done on your home and are completely satisfied with the result, you are considered to be one of the lucky ones. Because home improvements tend to be expensive and to cause some disruption while they are being carried out, we expect the finished product to be of a high standard. Unfortunately, many people are disappointed. The main problems are that:

- people are talked into having work done that they do not really want and perhaps cannot afford, by high-pressure doorstep salesmen
- there are rogues in the home improvement business who will take your money and run
- the firm goes out of business before the job is finished
- the firm is slow in completing the work

- the workmanship or materials are of poor quality
- there are unexpected increases in the cost.

How to avoid problems

* Never decide to have building work done on the spur of the moment merely because a contractor happens to have knocked on your door. The work may not really need doing and, even if it does, you should get a few quotations before you commit yourself (see Chapter 2, pages 22–6, for how to deal with doorstep salesmen).

* Get at least three written quotations. These should specify what will be done and what materials will be used. Don't necessarily accept the lowest quote. Ask yourself – and the builder – why he is so much cheaper than the rest. Is he inexperienced? Are his workmen or materials inferior? Will he later increase the price by finding extra work that needs doing? Is he a 'moon-lighter' with few overheads who will fit this job in when he can and may prove unreliable?

* If you are having major building work done, such as an extension, consider using an architect or surveyor. He will prepare plans and apply for planning permission, obtain quotations and advise on which contractor to choose and keep an eye on each stage of the work. Obviously there will be a fee for this service but an expert could prevent you making an expensive mistake. See Chapter 6, pages 121–3, for more on architects and Chapter 10, pages 195–7, for more on surveyors.

CHOOSING A FIRM
Before you pick a firm, follow the 'buy-laws':

☞ If you know anybody who has had similar work carried out recently, ask whether they would recommend the firm they used. If so, check that the firm will employ the *same team* on your home: many sub-contract their work to a number of different teams.

☞ If you are not going by personal recommendation, ask to see an example of the firm's work in your area – and talk to the home owners. If the firm raises objections to this, be wary.

☞ If possible, go for an established business and never use anybody unless you have their address and telephone number. Be wary of cards dropped through your letterbox which give only a name and telephone number.

☞ There are many trade associations in the home improvement field. Some may be little more than gangs of cowboys but others do offer consumers valuable protection such as guarantees against faulty workmanship (see above, pages 88–90, and below, page 94), for organisations worth contacting).

☞ Some firms offer long guarantees on their work in an attempt to convince you of their reliability. Do not be influenced by these. For one thing, the firm may go out of business, in which case the guarantee is useless unless it is protected by an insurance policy. For another, the terms of the guarantee may be very restricted and should be read carefully. Remember that a guarantee cannot take away your legal rights.

THE CONTRACT

Many problems over home improvements would be avoided if householders knew beforehand exactly what to expect. Get a written contract and **read it carefully**. If there is anything you are unhappy or uncertain about, check with the contractor. Take nothing for granted. The contract should include:

● a schedule of the work to be done. Problems often arise because householders think something has been included in the contract when it has not. If in doubt, ask. Make sure everything you want done is there in writing
● the exact cost of the work including labour, materials and VAT

- the name and address of the company carrying out the work
- the starting and finishing date
- details of cancellation rights, if any (see Chapter 2, page 27)
- details of the guarantee, if any.

PAYMENT

* Never hand over money in advance to a trader you know nothing about: he may well do a moonlight flit with your cash. Sometimes it is reasonable for a firm to ask for a deposit to cover the cost of materials. Only pay money in advance if you are satisfied that:

  - the firm is reputable and is an established business
  - the advance payment is to cover the cost of materials
  - the work is likely to be carried out.

* If you are using a local firm, you can ask to see an invoice for the cost of the materials from a builders' merchant before you settle up with the contractor. Builders' merchants usually give tradesmen free credit for a certain length of time and if your contractor cannot get materials on credit, it may mean his reputation is poor.

* If you need to make advance payments, use a cheque or credit card so you have some record of payment. Insist on a receipt with the firm's name and address on it. Some trade associations offer protection against lost deposits paid to their members (see below).

* Try to avoid paying for work 'as you go along' or you will lose your most effective lever against the firm. And *never* pay for more than the value of the work that has been done.

* Do not pay the final bill until you are completely satisfied. With major building work, it is wise to retain some of the payment until several months after the work is completed so you can see if any problems

develop; of course, you can only do this if your contract allows you to.

* Never sign a satisfaction note.

TRADE ASSOCIATIONS

The Building Employers' Confederation inspects the work of building firms applying for membership and – for a fee – will guarantee jobs costing £500–£30,000 against faulty workmanship or against the contractor going out of business before completing the work. This guarantee scheme only operates in England and Wales.

The Federation of Master Builders operates a register of warranted builders whose work is vetted. The warranty scheme also protects you if a member goes out of business while doing work for you and offers a guarantee against defects.

The Glass and Glazing Federation will reimburse customers for deposits paid to a member company that goes bust before completing the contract. Alternatively, the GGF will arrange for the work to be completed by another member.

Some firms offering damp course and wood treatment subscribe to the **Guaranteed Treatments Protection Trust,** which provides an insurance policy to back up its own guarantees. This means that if the firm offering the guarantee goes out of business, the consumer still has some protection.

The National Cavity Insulation Association operates a scheme which protects you if you have problems with insulation installed by a member firm which has subsequently gone out of business.

Renting and Hiring Goods
Companies that hire out goods are also performing a service – though of a rather different kind from those

discussed so far in this chapter. Whether you hire a car
or a carpet shampooer, rent a TV for five years or a DJ for
an evening, you are protected by the Supply of Goods
and Services Act. This says that goods which you hire,
rent or lease must be *as described*, *of merchantable quality*
and *fit for their purpose*. If they are not, you are entitled
to reject them and claim compensation.

Before you rent or hire goods, read the contract
carefully. Find out:

- what the hire charge is
- whether you have to pay a deposit
- when the payments have to be made
- who is responsible for repairs
- whether there are any conditions attached to the hire
- when you can end the agreement. The Consumer
  Credit Act 1974 says that you can pull out of a rental
  agreement after 18 months, regardless of what the
  contract says. However if the payments amount to
  more than £300 a year, you cannot pull out early unless
  the contract allows you to do so.

You must take reasonable care of any goods you rent
or hire and you will have to compensate the owner if
you lose or damage them. So you should enquire about
insurance when you hire the goods. You are not responsible for damage caused by fair wear and tear.

6

Professionals

Professionals have traditionally been treated rather differently from people providing the kinds of service I considered in the previous chapter. It is not hard to see why. The status and academic qualifications of people like doctors, solicitors and architects, the technical language they sometimes use, and the fact that you often consult them across a desk in their own offices can set them apart from their clients. It can be harder to 'shop around' for a professional than it is for a tradesman: you might find three plumbers on small jobs before you find one you like and trust, but you can hardly do the same with your doctor. And if you are unhappy with something a professional has done, you may lack the confidence to complain – or simply not know what steps to take.

Matters have improved recently. Many professions are now allowed to advertise – albeit in a restrained way – thus making them more accessible. Most professions are more conscious than they were of their public image and aware that they must give people what they want and be responsive to criticism.

Choosing and using a professional should not be like crossing the road blindfold. There are guidelines you can follow to help you get a good deal.

☞ **Remember!**
Professionals provide a service. You are entitled

to expect certain standards of them – as outlined in Chapter 5 – and to complain if those standards are not met.

Getting the Best out of a Professional

There are important differences between the way professionals and other contractors work. Being aware of these differences can prevent the misunderstandings which sometimes lead to suspicion and complaints.

* Charges are calculated in various ways – sometimes by the hour and sometimes for a specific piece of work. Do not be afraid to ask about fees in advance. A professional may not be able to give you a firm quotation for every job, because he may not know in advance how much work is involved, but he will be able to give a rough estimate and to explain how his fees are calculated.

* You cannot always *see* what a professional is doing as you can with, say, a builder or a hairdresser. That is why his bill may come as a shock. Do not be afraid to ask what is going on behind the scenes. If you are unhappy about the bill, ask for an explanation.

* If a professional uses language you do not understand, ask for clarification.

* Unlike other kinds of contractor, who may or may not belong to a trade association with a code of conduct, professionals are bound by the rules of their professional body which are intended to protect consumers. This means, among other things, that they must have professional indemnity insurance: if you suffer loss or injury because of the incompetence of a professional and successfully sue him for negligence, you will get your money.

* There are recognised procedures for dealing with every type of complaint in every profession. Of course some

procedures are simpler to follow and work better from the consumer's point of view than others.

Doctors

Choosing a GP
Finding out the names and addresses of GPs in your area is relatively easy. There are lists at offices of the Family Practitioner Committee (you will find the address under that title in the telephone directory or on the front of your medical card) and at your local Community Health Council (under that title in the telephone directory). You will probably also find a list at main post offices, libraries and Citizens' Advice Bureaux, though it may not be completely up to date. Some lists give only the most basic information; others include surgery hours, whether there is an appointments system and details of clinics run at the surgery.

Finding a practice which suits you is a little more difficult. Ask friends and neighbours whether they would recommend their own GP and – equally important – whether there are any GPs in the area they would avoid. Chemists may also be helpful.

When you have narrowed down the choice, visit a few surgeries to see what the surroundings and facilities are like. Some practices have leaflets describing their services which you can take away. If you are considering joining a GP's list, you can ask to meet the doctor for an informal chat. Some doctors are happy to do this; others are not – their reaction to this suggestion alone reveals something about them.

There are various questions to ask before you register with a doctor. Getting the answers to these will reduce the risk of your ending up with a practice you dislike. Find out:

- whether the practice operates an appointments system and, if so, how quickly you can usually see a doctor. If there is no appointments system find out how long you normally have to wait at the surgery. Some practices operate a dual system, with appointments for some surgeries and 'queuing' for others.

- what the surgery hours are. Do they suit you? If you find it difficult to take time off work, ask what is the latest you can visit the surgery in the evening. Is there a Saturday surgery and, if so, is it for emergencies only?
- how many doctors there are in the practice. If it is a group practice, can you see any doctor you choose or are you expected to stick to your own? You may prefer to see your own doctor all the time – is this feasible? And what happens if you find you prefer one of the other members of the practice? If the age and sex of your GP is important to you, find out about this.
- who does home visits in the evenings and at weekends. When your GP is not on duty, another doctor must be available. Sometimes the cover is provided by other doctors in the practice or by doctors in another practice nearby. Some doctors pay to use a deputising service which sends one of a panel of doctors to you when you call. If you prefer to see a familiar face when you call a doctor, then the practice's off-duty arrangements will matter to you.
- whether you can get to the surgery easily and – if you drive – park nearby.
- what the waiting area is like. If you have children, are there toys for them to play with? If so, it suggests the practice is well used to dealing with mothers and children.
- whether the receptionist is approachable and friendly.
- whether the practice runs any clinics such as ante-natal, well-woman or baby clinics. If not, where will you go for these? If the practice is in a health centre, you will generally find other facilities on the premises such as a nurse, health visitor and chiropodist. How important is it to you to have these services 'on the spot'?

Registering with a GP
Once you have found a practice you like, take your medical card along to the surgery (or, if you do not have a medical card, ask for a registration card when you get there) and find out whether you can join their list. No

doctor is obliged to take you unless told to do so by the
Family Practitioner Committee. If you have difficulty in
finding a doctor, contact the FPC, which will allocate
you to a practice.

Changing your GP

You can change your GP for any reason and you do not
have to say why. First, find another who will accept
you. Then get your present GP to sign your medical
card, or, if you prefer, send it to the FPC explaining that
you wish to transfer doctors.

A doctor can remove you from his list without giving
a reason, although he must not do so while you are
having a course of treatment. If your doctor removes
you from his list, you will be told by the FPC, which
must make sure you are not left without a GP.

Although in theory there is nothing to stop you
changing doctors as often as you like, in practice you
may find if you swap too frequently that you gain a
reputation as a troublemaker and have difficulty per-
suading a doctor to take you voluntarily. This is why it
is so important to find out as much as you can about
your doctor and his practice *before* you register.

Private medical care

When you are registered with a GP on the NHS you
cannot see him privately and he must not ask you to
pay for a consultation or visit. He can make a charge for
some services such as issuing an international certificate of vaccination or a medical certificate for your
employers, signing a passport form and giving you a
check up for insurance or other purposes.

If your GP decides to refer you to a specialist, you
may decide that you want to pay to go privately. The
advantage of a private consultation is that for non-
urgent problems you will usually be able to see a doctor
more quickly, you will be given more time – though not
a 'better service' – in a more relaxed atmosphere and
without having to queue in a hospital waiting room. If
you need several consultations, you will always see the

same specialist. While you are receiving private treatment, you can at any time switch to the NHS, though of course you cannot insist upon seeing the same consultant.

If you have private medical insurance, check before you have any kind of private treatment that you are covered for the charge that will be made. Do not be afraid to ask a consultant's secretary about his charges. Most consultants charge on a time basis. In general you will pay more to see somebody who works in one of the specialist medical districts, like Harley Street in London, because overheads there are very high.

Complaining about your GP

How you make a complaint about your GP depends on the nature of the problem.

Complaints that the GP may have breached his **terms of service** are dealt with by the FPC. If your doctor suggested he should see you privately, for a fee, to discuss your treatment in more detail, or refused to visit your sick child when this was necessary, these would be matters for the FPC.

* Write to the FPC within eight weeks of the event which provoked the complaint. The FPC may try to resolve the matter informally, perhaps by talking separately to you and the GP.

* If this does not work, or is not appropriate, the FPC will tell you whether it can investigate the matter formally. If so, a service committee will be formed consisting of doctors and lay people. The chairman of the service committee will consider your complaint first and make a recommendation to the full committee. If he thinks the doctor may have broken his terms of service, he will seek the doctor's views and give you a chance to comment on them. A hearing may be held at which you can call witnesses. You can present your own case or somebody else may do this for you, as long as you do not pay them.

* If the service committee decides that the doctor has broken his terms of service, the FPC will recommend what action should be taken. He may be given a warning or some of his salary may be stopped.

* Either you or the doctor can appeal against the decision to the Secretary of State for Social Services. The FPC will explain how to do this.

There are no FPCs in Scotland or Northern Ireland. In Scotland, complaints are dealt with by the area health board and in Northern Ireland by the Central Services Agency.

Complaints about **professional misconduct** are dealt with by the General Medical Council. If your doctor made an improper suggestion to you, was drunk in surgery, or disclosed confidential information about you without your permission, these would be matters for the GMC.

* If the GMC thinks the complaint deserves investigation, it will refer the matter to its Professional Conduct Committee, which will consider it in detail. It can take statements, convene a formal hearing and may take action ranging from a warning to the GP to striking his name off the medical register, thus preventing him from practising.

* If the doctor's physical or mental health seems to be adversely affecting his work, the GMC's Health Committee may investigate.

Complaints about hospitals

* If you want to make a complaint whilst in hospital, raise it with the ward sister who will report it to somebody more senior. The hospital administrator is responsible for the hospital's services and the consultant in charge of your case for your medical treatment.

* You can if you prefer, or if you have left hospital, write to the administrator of the district health authority, who will investigate and take the matter up with the relevant people and report back to you. The ward sister or local Community Health Council or Citizens' Advice Bureau will give you the address. In Scotland contact the area health board, and in Northern Ireland the Central Services Agency.

* If your complaint is about medical treatment, it is up to the consultant in charge of your case to try to sort the matter out. He may offer to meet you at this stage.

* If you get nowhere, write again either to the consultant or to the district administrator outlining your complaint and explaining why you are still dissatisfied. The consultant may offer to discuss the matter again with you. Alternatively, your case may be referred for a 'second opinion' to two independent consultants who will convene a meeting with all the parties to discuss the problem. They will then report to the Regional Medical Officer on what action should be taken to ensure the problem does not arise again. This procedure is intended to be used in cases that are serious but are unlikely to lead to a negligence claim.

THE HEALTH SERVICE COMMISSIONER (OMBUDSMAN)
The Health Service Commissioner can investigate complaints about health service administration but not about medical treatment. He cannot deal with complaints about GPs. If you have written to the district administrator and are not satisfied with the reply, write to the Commissioner and you will be told whether he can investigate your complaint. The district health authority, Community Health Council or Citizens' Advice Bureau can give you a leaflet explaining what the Commissioner does and how his office works.

Negligence
None of the complaints procedures described so far

will help you to obtain compensation for any distress, injury or suffering caused as a result of medical treatment. If it is financial compensation you want, you will have to sue for negligence, through the courts. You may be able to obtain legal aid for this (see below, page 116).

Your local CAB or CHC will give you advice on what to do and may be able to suggest a solicitor who specialises in medical negligence cases. Action for the Victims of Medical Accidents can also help you to find a specialist solicitor.

☞ Before you embark on this road, **be warned.** Suing for medical negligence is a long and complicated process, which can be very expensive if you do not qualify for legal aid. It can be hard to find one doctor to testify against another. You then have to prove that the doctor you are suing did not exercise reasonable care and skill in carrying out the operation or treatment. You will need a good deal of patience, determination and energy.

Dentists

Finding a dentist
You will find a list of dentists who do NHS work at the offices of the Family Practitioner Committee and the local Community Health Council. There may also be a list at main post offices, libraries and Citizens' Advice Bureaux. Ask your GP, friends and neighbours if they can recommend a dentist. As you will probably visit your dentist less often than your doctor, you may be prepared to travel further to see one with a good reputation. Before you choose, find out:

- what the surgery times are. Are there evening or Saturday morning appointments?
- how long you have to wait for an appointment
- whether there is an emergency service for urgent cases
- what the surgery and waiting room are like
- whether the dentist is good with children
- whether he does the full range of NHS work.

Sometimes it can be difficult to find a dentist who will do the full range of NHS work including dentures, crowns and bridges. The Family Practitioner Committee may be able to give you the names of dentists in your area who do complex work on the NHS. Dentists are now allowed to advertise and can include this kind of information in their ads. If you cannot find an NHS dentist willing to do the work you need, you may have to look further afield or consider private treatment.

NHS or private?

Everybody is entitled to free check-ups on the NHS. Pregnant women and those who have had a baby within the last year, young people under 19 in full-time education and some people on low incomes are entitled to completely free NHS dental treatment. Young people aged 16–18 who have left school can get everything free except dentures and bridges. Everybody else has to pay the full cost of treatment up to a certain sum and then a proportion of the cost over that sum.

Problems sometimes arise because not everybody realises that you do not register with a dentist as you do with a doctor. Instead, you make a new contract with him each time you sign an NHS form for a new course of treatment. Just because the dentist has given you one course of treatment on the NHS, does not mean he has to see you on the NHS in future. For this reason it is wise to check before you start each course of treatment that it is on the NHS.

Once a dentist accepts you for NHS treatment he must do everything necessary to render you 'dentally fit'. He cannot mix private and NHS treatment. So he would be in breach of his terms of service if he told you, in the middle of a course of treatment, that you needed a gold filling, but that he could only do this privately.

When the dentist has established what needs to be done to make you dentally fit, he should tell you what the treatment will cost and is entitled to ask for payment in advance.

There has been some concern about dentists doing unnecessary work. A 1986 government report con-

firmed that there was a 'small but significant and un-
acceptable amount of deliberate unnecessary treatment
in the General Dental Service' and suggested solutions
to the problem. If you are concerned that your dentist
may be suggesting work that is unnecessary, seek a
second opinion.

Emergency treatment
Unlike doctors, dentists do not have to provide emergency cover at all hours. If you need treatment out of
hours, try your own dentist first. Otherwise try any
dentist. But check whether you will be seen on the NHS
or privately. There is no NHS charge for calling a
dentist out to his surgery in an emergency, but unless
you are one of those entitled to free dental treatment
you will have to pay for any treatment you receive.
Some health authorities have set up NHS emergency
services. The FPC will tell you whether there is such a
scheme in your area. If you cannot contact a dentist,
your GP or the accident and emergency department at a
hospital will give you something to stop bleeding or
reduce severe pain.

Complaining about a dentist

* If you have a complaint about poor NHS dental treatment, try to sort it out with your dentist first. If he
  cannot resolve the problem, contact the FPC within six
  months of the end of the treatment or eight weeks
  after you noticed the cause of complaint, whichever is
  sooner (see above, pages 101–2, for what to do).

  If the Service Committee agrees that the dentist has
  broken his **terms of service**, it may recommend that he
  reimburses you for money you spent correcting his
  mistakes but it will not award any other compensation.

* If you have a complaint about private dental treatment,
  your only option at present is to take the dentist to
  court. If he has not carried out the treatment with
  reasonable care and skill, at a reasonable charge (unless

you agreed a price beforehand) and within a reasonable time, you may have a case against him under the Supply of Goods and Services Act (see above, pages 71–7). If you have suffered injury because of your dentist's incompetence, you may have a case against him for negligence (see above, page 103). You will have to find a solicitor who specialises in this kind of work, and a dental expert prepared to testify against your own dentist. The British Dental Association is currently considering whether to set up an arbitration procedure for complaints about private dental treatment.

* If your complaint is about **professional misconduct** by a dentist, write to the General Dental Council. If there appears to be a case against the dentist, the Preliminary Proceedings Committee will investigate and decide on the basis of written evidence whether to refer the matter to a full public enquiry before the Professional Conduct Committee.

Opticians

The way you choose and buy glasses has changed a good deal recently. Anybody can now call themselves an optician, whether they are qualified or not. However if they are not registered with the General Optical Council or supervised by somebody who is, they must make this clear – by saying 'Optician (unregistered)' for example.

The people involved in testing sight, prescribing and dispensing glasses trade under a multitude of different names.

An **optometrist** or **ophthalmic optician** can test sight, prescribe and dispense spectacles. He may have an extra qualification in contact lens practice.

An **ophthalmic medical practitioner** is a doctor who can test sight and prescribe spectacles or contact lenses. He does not usually dispense.

A **registered dispensing optician** is qualified to supply spectacles but not to test sight. He may work with an optometrist or in separate dispensing premises.

A **spectacle shop** can also dispense. Some have qualified staff on the premises to check that your prescription has been made up correctly; others do not. Unqualified staff are not allowed to dispense to certain categories of spectacle wearers (see below).

An **unregistered optician** with no qualifications can dispense spectacles (but not contact lenses) to anybody who presents a prescription less than two years old, except children under 16, or registered blind or partially sighted people.

Finding an optician
You will find a list of opticians who do NHS work at the offices of the Family Practitioner Committee and the local Community Health Council. There may also be a list at main post offices, libraries and Citizens' Advice Bureaux. Registered opticians are allowed to advertise, giving basic information about their services.

Opticians tend to work in the high street, so you can see what their premises and range of spectacles are like without committing yourself. Do not be too influenced by prices in shop windows: some opticians display prices for lenses and frames, others for frames only. Obviously the appearance of the shop and its stock will give you no clue as to the quality of the optician's work. Once again, the best advice is to go by recommendation.

☞ **Remember!**
You do not have to buy your spectacles where you have your sight test (see below).

NHS or private?
Everybody is entitled to a free NHS sight test once a year or more often if clinically necessary. Children under 16, students under 19 in full-time education,

some people on low incomes and those who need
particularly powerful or complex lenses are entitled to a
voucher which can be put towards the cost of private
glasses. There are no longer any NHS glasses. Everybody else has to pay the full cost of private glasses.

After you have had a sight test, you must be given a
prescription whether or not your sight has altered. If
you need new glasses you may buy them from the
person who tested your sight or you can take your
prescription elsewhere. Do not feel obliged to buy
where you had your sight tested. You are free to shop
around until you find a frame you like at a price you can
afford: prices do vary considerably.

If you do not want to spend a great deal, find an
optician with a budget range.

Complaining about an optician

* If you are unhappy about some aspect of your treat-
  ment, try to sort the matter out with your optician.
  * If you simply cannot get used to your new glasses,
    ask the dispenser to check that your prescription
    has been correctly made up. If it has, you can ask the
    FPC for permission to have another sight test.
  * If you have a complaint about the quality of your
    glasses, remember that spectacles are goods. Under
    the Sale of Goods Act 1979 they should be *as
    described, of merchantable quality* and *fit for their
    purpose*. If yours are not, you are entitled to a refund
    or compensation (see Chapter 3).

* If you cannot sort your complaint out with the optician,
  write to the FPC within eight weeks of the problem
  arising (see above, pages 101–2, for what to do). Alternatively, you can contact the Consumer Complaints
  Service at the Association of Optical Practitioners. The
  AOP will mediate in disputes between its members
  and their patients. If the optician concerned does not
  belong to the AOP, your complaint will be forwarded to
  the appropriate organisation.

* Complaints about **professional misconduct** by a registered optician should be sent to the General Optical Council or, in the case of ophthalmic medical practitioners, to the General Medical Council.

* If you have suffered injury because of your optician's incompetence, you may have a case against him for negligence (see above, page 103).

Pharmacists

The pharmacist can be a valuable source of advice on health care and may be able to save you a visit to the doctor when you have a minor ailment.

Buying medicines
There are three groups of medicines:

● medicines you can buy in a pharmacy or in a supermarket, drug store, etc. The mild painkillers fall into this category. If you want to save money on this kind of drug, buy the unbranded version – it will have BP or BPC after its name – rather than one of the much-advertised branded lines. It may vary slightly, but the main active ingredient will be the same.
● medicines you can obtain with or without a prescription from a pharmacy only. If you are given a prescription for one of these drugs and do not qualify for free prescriptions (see below), check with the pharmacist whether it would be cheaper to pay the prescription charge or to buy the drug 'over the counter'. Which method is cheaper may depend on the quantity on the prescription.
● medicines available on prescription only.

When you obtain a new drug ask the pharmacist:

* what it is for
* whether it has any side-effects
* when you should take it and in what dose
* where you should store it

* whether it is important that you should complete the course.

Free prescriptions
There are no prescription charges for men over 65 and women over 60, children under 16, pregnant women and those who have had a baby in the last year, some people on low incomes, those suffering from certain specific conditions including diabetes and epilepsy and also war or service pensioners needing prescriptions for their disability. The birth control pill is also free.

Out-of-hours supplies
In most areas chemists operate a rota to ensure that you can get your prescription made up after normal shop hours and at some time on Sundays and Bank Holidays. Details of which pharmacist is on duty are displayed in chemists' windows and doors, and may be available from the police or printed in local newspapers.

Emergency supplies
It is up to you to make sure you do not run out of drugs you rely on. If you do, and you cannot get a prescription from the doctor, you may be able to find a pharmacist who will provide enough medication to tide you over until the next surgery. He will only do so if, after speaking to you, he is satisfied that the emergency is genuine, that the medication has been prescribed for you by a doctor before and that the drug is not one of those which he is forbidden under any circumstances to dispense without a prescription.

Complaining about a pharmacist

* If you have a complaint, try to resolve the matter with the pharmacist himself.

* If you cannot sort the matter out, write to the FPC within eight weeks of the incident which provoked the complaint (see above, pages 101–2, for what to do).

* Alternatively, you can write to the Pharmaceutical Society of Great Britain. They investigate complaints of incompetence as well as **professional misconduct.**

* If you have suffered injury because of a pharmacist's incompetence you may have a case against him for negligence (see above, page 103).

Alternative Medicine

While there are controls over who may call themselves a doctor, dentist, registered optician or pharmacist, anybody can set up as an osteopath, acupuncturist, hypnotherapist, psychotherapist or homoeopath. This means you may be treated by somebody with specialist qualifications and training or somebody who opened up in practice the week before after a lifetime as a milkman.

You can protect yourself from the latter kind by sticking to practitioners who are registered with one of the professional organisations which supervise training and qualifications. Some doctors have additional qualifications in alternative medicine, though few give this kind of treatment on the NHS.

The Institute of Complementary Medicine can advise you on how to find a qualified practitioner in any of 50 different therapies.

Getting help

Community Health Councils

CHCs are useful sources of information and advice on all matters involving the health service. They can tell you about facilities in your area, explain how to pursue a complaint and may accompany you to a hearing of your complaint, though not to court.

The Scottish equivalent of the CHC is the local health

council; the equivalent in Northern Ireland is the district committee.

The Patients' Association
The Patients' Association can give you information on the health care services – private and NHS. It will advise on anything from changing your GP to complaining about your optician and produces a number of useful leaflets.

Accountants

Finding an accountant
Anybody can set up in business as an accountant with no qualifications or training. The Yellow Pages list those in your area. If you want an accountant who is fully trained, choose one with a recognised qualification. The main organisations involved in the training of accountants for private practice (as opposed to business and industry) are The Institute of Chartered Accountants in England and Wales and the Chartered Association of Certified Accountants.

Only accountants who have passed the exams set by the first and its sister bodies in Scotland and Ireland may call themselves chartered accountants. They use the initials FCA or ACA after their name. Only those who have passed the exams set by the second may call themselves certified accountants. They use the initials FCCA or ACCA after their name. There are more chartered than certified accountants and a higher proportion of them are in private practice.

Each of these bodies can supply a list of their members in your area. Some accountants advertise and this may help you to choose one, but personal recommendation is the best guide. Your bank or building society manager may be able to suggest a firm. Firms of accountants tend not to specialise as much as solicitors so, unless you have a very complicated or unusual problem, most practices should be able to help you.

Getting financial advice

Many firms of accountants will give you a free first
interview at which you can discuss your requirements
or the nature of your problem and get an idea of what the
firm would charge to deal with it. When you telephone
for an appointment, ask whether there is a charge for this
preliminary meeting.

Do not be afraid to discuss fees at the outset. An
accountant will not necessarily be able to give you a firm
quotation, but he should give you an idea of what a
specific job will cost or what his hourly charges are.

Many Citizens' Advice Bureaux have a panel of
accountants who will give financial advice free of charge
at CAB offices.

Complaining about an accountant

* If you have a complaint about the way an accountant has
  handled your affairs, try to sort the matter out with the
  firm itself by writing to one of the senior partners (their
  names are at the top of the list on the headed notepaper)
  outlining the problem clearly and concisely.

* If you are unhappy with his response, write to the
  Investigations Committee at the accountant's professional body. Your complaint might concern:

  ● fees
  ● slowness in dealing with your affairs
  ● not replying to letters
  ● incompetence.

  The Investigations Committee at the professional body
  concerned will look into your complaint and ask the
  accountant for his comments. If you appear to have a
  justifiable complaint, it will refer the matter for full
  investigation to the Disciplinary Committee, which has
  the power to fine a member or suspend or bar him from
  membership.

* If your complaint concerns the fees charged by a
  chartered accountant and cannot be resolved by the

Institute of which he is a member, you can request that an arbitrator be appointed whose decision will be binding.

* The professional bodies have no power to award compensation. If you think your accountant has not done his job with reasonable care and skill, at a reasonable charge (unless a fee was agreed) or within a reasonable time, you may have claim against him under the Supply of Goods and Services Act (see Chapter 5, pages 71–7). If you think you have suffered financial loss as a result of an accountant's incompetence, you will have to consider suing him for negligence.

Solicitors

Finding a solicitor

You will find a list of solicitors in the Yellow Pages and in the Solicitors' Directory at libraries. However solicitors do a wide variety of work and these lists give you no information to assess whether a firm is likely to suit your needs. The Solicitors' Regional Directory, available at libraries and Citizens' Advice Bureaux, lists firms of solicitors county by county indicating the kind of work each firm is willing to undertake – for example, consumer cases, employment, housing and legal aid. CABs usually have a good working relationship with local firms and will be able to suggest solicitors who specialise in the kind of job you have in mind. They can also make an appointment for you and give you a letter of introduction. Your bank or building society manager may also be able to recommend a solicitor.

Before you choose a firm of solicitors find out:

● whether they are experienced in the kind of problem you have
● whether they do legal aid work – firms that handle legal aid work display a special logo in their windows
● whether they give a fixed-fee first interview (see below)
● whether they do emergency work out of hours.

Getting legal advice

* Many solicitors offer a half-hour first interview for a fixed fee of £5. This can be useful in helping you to decide whether to take your case further.

* If you are on a low income you may qualify for legal aid, in which case all or part of your legal costs will be paid. There are two aspects to legal aid for civil cases: whether you qualify for either depends on the size of your income and what assets you have – including your home. You can get a leaflet outlining the financial limits from CABs, law centres or solicitors who do legal aid work or from the Law Society's Publications Department.

  • Under the **green form scheme** (called the pink form scheme in Scotland) you can get a limited amount of free legal advice with relatively little red tape.
  • Getting **civil legal aid** – in order to take a case to court for example – is more complicated and takes longer as the DHSS has to look into your finances and decide whether you qualify. You will have to pay for any work done before your application is approved, or ask your solicitor to delay starting work on the case until legal aid is granted. In some circumstances you can get emergency legal aid.

When you consult a solicitor:

* Find out what he is likely to charge for dealing with your problem and how his fees are calculated.

* Sort out any documents relating to your case and bring these to your first interview, assembled tidily in chronological order.

* Do not be afraid to chase him to find out what is going on, but do not phone or visit him unnecessarily – time costs money.

FREE LEGAL ADVICE

* Many CABs operate rota schemes where local solicitors see people by appointment for a short interview at the bureau, generally in the evenings. The solicitor will give advice free of charge and may be able to help you sort out a simple problem on the spot. But the main aim of these interviews is for you to find out whether you need the help of a solicitor, what courses of action are open to you and what they would involve. If you need further help you can visit the solicitor as a client in his own office, but of course you will have to pay or make an application for legal aid. In some areas, CABs provide free legal advice on a slightly different basis.

* Law centres also provide free legal advice. However, there are only 57 of these covering only one-tenth of the country – mostly the major cities – and you cannot consult a law centre outside your own area. A solicitor at a law centre will give the same kind of 'diagnostic' interview as a CAB rota solicitor. He may well refer you to a solicitor in private practice and will know which firms in the area specialise in your kind of problem. Alternatively, if you cannot afford to see a solicitor privately and your problem is one that does not qualify for legal aid, law centre staff may act for you at no charge. Law centres do not do conveyancing, probate, personal injury claims over £2,000, crime or commercial work.

EMERGENCY WORK
Anybody who is held as a suspect at a police station is entitled to see a solicitor free of charge. You will be handed a notice explaining how to get a solicitor. You can name your own solicitor, if he does this kind of work, or ask the police to call an independent 24-hour duty solicitor.

Complaining about a solicitor

OVERCHARGING

* Tell your solicitor if you think his bill is too high. He may be prepared to reduce it.

* If the bill is for a job which did not involve court work – the sale and purchase of property for example – you can ask the solicitor to apply for a **remuneration certificate** from the Law Society. He must tell you about your right to seek a certificate before he can sue you for not paying your bill and must give you 28 days to apply for one. A panel of solicitors appointed by the Law Society will consider the work that was done, the fee charged and your comments and will issue a certificate stating what a reasonable charge would be: it will not increase the bill – only confirm or reduce it.

    There is no remuneration certificate procedure in Scotland. However, the Law Society of Scotland will informally scrutinise a solicitor's bill.

* If the work involved a court case, you can ask for the bill to be **taxed** by the court. This procedure – which has nothing at all to do with Inland Revenue taxation – is more complicated and will cost you money. You will have to pay court fees and – unless the court decides to cut your bill by a fifth or more – the cost of the taxation itself and any extra costs your solicitor has incurred in drawing up a bill for taxation purposes. The taxation office at court will explain how to apply.

OTHER COMPLAINTS

* If you are dissatisfied with some aspect of your solicitor's work, try to sort the matter out with the firm itself by putting your complaint in writing to one of the senior partners (their names are at the top of the list on the firm's headed notepaper).

* There has been much controversy in recent years about the procedure for handling complaints against solici-

tors. As a result changes have been made, but it remains
to be seen whether these actually improve matters.
Instead of complaints being investigated by a Law
Society committee, they are now dealt with by the
Solicitors' Complaints Bureau. But as this is funded by
the Law Society some people remain sceptical of its in-
dependence. The Bureau deals with complaints about:

- poor workmanship, incompetence and inefficiency
- overcharging
- delays in answering your letters or enquiries
- delay in dealing with your case
- dishonesty and deception
- acting in the same case for you and somebody else
  whose interest conflicts with yours
- failure to deal with your money properly
- failure to hand over your papers if you have asked
  for them and do not owe the solicitor any money.

Write to the Bureau explaining the nature of your
complaint. The Bureau will ask your solicitor for his
comments and may refer your case to its Adjudication
Committee for a full investigation. The committee has
the power to discipline the solicitor by fining him,
suspending him from practising for a time or striking
him off the roll of solicitors. It can also order the
solicitor to repay all or part of his fees to you. Very
serious allegations of professional misconduct – such
as embezzling clients' money – would be heard by
the independent Solicitors' Disciplinary Tribunal; of
course this would also be a matter for the police.

---

* If you are unhappy about the way the Bureau has dealt
with your complaint, you can write to the Lay Observer
within three months of the announcement of the
Bureau's decision. The job of the Lay Observer – who is
not a lawyer – is to make sure your complaint has been
fully and fairly investigated by the Bureau. If he decides
that it has not been dealt with fairly or that a further
investigation should be carried out, he will ask the
Bureau to look at your case again. This happens in a
tiny minority of cases.

There are separate Law Societies for Scotland and
Northern Ireland with different complaints procedures. Scotland and Northern Ireland also have their
own Lay Observers.

TAKING YOUR SOLICITOR TO COURT
The procedures described above may result in your
getting some of your fees back, but they will not bring
you any other financial compensation.

* If you think your solicitor has not done his job with
  reasonable care and skill, at a reasonable charge (unless
  the fee was agreed beforehand) or within a reasonable
  time, you may have a claim against him under the
  Supply of Goods and Services Act (see above, pages
  71–7).

* If you have suffered financial loss as a result of your
  solicitor's incompetence, you may be able to sue him
  for negligence.

  • If your negligence claim is a fairly small one and can
    be dealt with in writing without a hearing, you can
    make use of the Solicitors' Arbitration Scheme run
    by the Chartered Institute of Arbitrators. You can
    only do this if the solicitor agrees (which makes
    this scheme different from most others run by the
    Institute). If you lose, you cannot normally take the
    solicitor to court. See Chapter 13 for more detail on
    arbitration: the Solicitors' Arbitration Scheme
    works much like Code of Practice Arbitration
    schemes. It does not cover solicitors practising in
    Scotland or Northern Ireland.
  • If you decide to go to court rather than arbitration,
    you must find a solicitor willing to act for you; this
    can be difficult. The Law Society has a panel of
    solicitors who will advise you on whether you have
    a case: a member of the panel will give you up to an
    hour free of charge and will then be willing to act for
    you if you decide to go ahead.

Barristers

Sometimes your solicitor will seek the advice of a barrister, who may then represent you if the case goes to court.

* If you are unhappy about some aspect of your barrister's work, tell your solicitor who may take the matter up for you.

* If he gets nowhere, write to your barrister's Head of Chambers – the equivalent of the senior partner in a professional firm. The Chambers system does not operate in Scotland and Northern Ireland.

* If you still have no success, write to the barristers' professional body, the Bar Council, setting out clearly all the relevant facts relating to your case and your complaint. The Council's Professional Conduct Committee will consider your case and may reprimand or discipline the barrister if appropriate. It cannot award you compensation.

* If your complaint concerns your barrister's appearance in court, there is little you can do: you cannot sue a barrister over his advocacy work. If you feel he has given you bad advice, you may have a case against him for negligence.

* One of the most frequent complaints about the Bar is that the barrister dealing with your case is 'double booked' on the day of your trial and another barrister from the same chambers – who may only have read the papers the night before – takes over at the last minute. This is common practice and there is nothing you can do about it.

Architects

Finding an architect

Anybody calling themselves an architect must have certain qualifications and be registered with the Architects'

Registration Council of the United Kingdom (ARCUK), so if you pick somebody out of the Yellow Pages you can be confident that he is professionally qualified. However, architects do a vast range of work and you will not need or want a firm specialising in designing airports to draw up plans for your loft conversion. The Clients' Advisory Service of the Royal Institute of British Architects can give you the names of local architects doing the kind of work you have in mind. Local surveyors, estate agents and builders may be able to help. And ask friends who have used an architect recently whether they would recommend him. Once you have found an architect who seems to fit the bill, ask to see work of a similar type that he has done and to talk to the homeowners.

An architect will:

* discuss ideas with you
* draw up plans and apply for planning permission and building regulations consent
* invite builders to tender for the work
* plan the project
* supervise operations while the work is being done.

An architect may charge a percentage of the total cost of the building work or he may calculate his fees according to the services you will require of him. Find out about fees in advance.

Complaining about an architect

* If you are dissatisfied with some aspect of your architect's work, try to sort the problem out with the firm itself by writing to one of the senior partners (their names are at the top of the list on the firm's headed notepaper) setting out your complaint clearly and concisely.

* If you are still not satisfied, and the architect belongs to the Royal Institute of British Architects, write outlining your complaint to RIBA's Professional Conduct Com-

mittee, which will investigate and report back to you.
RIBA deals with complaints against its members involving:

- dishonesty or lack of integrity
- improper conduct of a client's affairs or failure to
  consult a client
- breach of confidentiality
- failure to tell the client about other interests which
  conflict with the client's
- obtaining commissions improperly.

The Royal Incorporation of Architects in Scotland,
and the Royal Society of Ulster Architects will investigate complaints against their members in Scotland and
Northern Ireland.

---

* If you think your architect is guilty of **disgraceful
conduct** – which in practice usually means committing
a criminal offence – you should report him to ARCUK.

---

* None of these bodies has power to award compensation. If your architect has not performed his job with
reasonable care and skill, at a reasonable charge (unless
a fee was agreed beforehand) or within a reasonable
time, you may have a claim against him under the
Supply of Goods and Services Act (see above, pages
71–7). If your architect has caused damage to your
property or injury to you because of his incompetence,
you may have a case against him for negligence.

Estate Agents and Surveyors
For information on how to choose, deal with and complain about estate agents and surveyors, see Chapter
10.

7

Public Services

We all grumble about public services – about the phone
that has been out of order for a week, the first class letter
which took a fortnight to arrive, our vastly overestimated electricity meter reading.

We all grouse, but we rarely do more. People seem
smitten with a feeling of impotence when it comes
to dealing with the corporations that provide public
services. Perhaps the fact that these corporations are
generally monopolies makes us feel it is useless to
complain because we know that *they* know that we
cannot take our business elsewhere. Perhaps we feel
intimidated by large organisations. Perhaps we simply
do not know where and how to register our dissatisfaction.

If you have a problem concerning a public service,
report it. Persistence pays when you are dealing with a
large organisation, and if you think you have a justified
complaint, do not let yourself be fobbed off. Most of the
utilities have formal procedures for dealing with complaints and are monitored by consumer 'watchdog'
bodies which will give advice and investigate on your
behalf.

When dealing with a public service, follow these
rules:

☞ Always keep your bills. That way you can make comparisons and will have the evidence to back up your case if one bill seems inexplicably high.

☞ Mark on each bill how, when and where you paid in case there is any dispute about this.

☞ If you have a query about your bill, or cannot afford to pay it, write to or telephone the local office named on the bill *immediately*. Do not ignore the problem in the hope that it will go away – it won't. And the organisation concerned is much more likely to be sympathetic if you are open with them from the start.

☞ If you have a complaint, put it in writing, keeping a copy, and address it to the right person (try to find out first, by telephone, who this is). State the problem, clearly, concisely and calmly: anger only generates more anger. Refer to how delighted you have been with the corporation's service in the past and how disappointed you are at the present lapse.

☞ Make a note of the name of the person handling your complaint and the department in which he works so that you can contact him again if you need to.

☞ If you are confident of your case, don't give in. If there is a possibility you may be right, public services will often give you the benefit of the doubt.

Gas and Electricity
Most people receive a gas and/or electricity bill every quarter. If you find it difficult to pay this all at once, you have various options. You can pay for fuel by:

● **pre-payment, coin-in-the-slot meter.** This means you don't get any fuel unless you pay for it in advance – so it is impossible to run up a big bill. The drawbacks are that you need to keep a supply of coins handy and that paying for fuel this way can work out more expensive than if you have an ordinary credit meter. Also, if the meter is broken into and the money stolen, you may have to repay it to the gas or electricity board. If the board does not think this kind of meter is safe or practical, it can refuse to install one.

- **cashless pre-payment meters.** Token-operated meters are being installed in some areas. Their main advantage is that there is no money to be stolen.

- **monthly budget payments.** The gas region or electricity board works out how much fuel you are likely to use over the year and spreads the cost over ten or 12 equal monthly instalments – so you won't receive a huge quarterly bill at the end of the winter. Financially you'd be better off if you put the money aside yourself into a building society account where it could earn interest for you until the quarterly bill arrived; but you might be tempted to raid the account in the meantime.

- **savings stamps.** You can buy these when you like from gas and electricity showrooms and some post offices and use them towards your quarterly bill.

Disconnections
If you cannot pay your gas or electricity bill, let the appropriate region or board know immediately. The gas and electricity industries have a code of practice on disconnections and will not cut off your supply if:

* you agree upon and stick to an arrangement for paying what you owe by instalments over a set period. If you miss a payment, the board can disconnect you without further warning.

* it is safe and practical to instal a slot meter. This will be set to collect the money you owe as well as the cost of the fuel you are using.

* it is between October 1st and March 31st and all the people in the house are old age pensioners.

* the debt is in the name of a past customer and you have made proper arrangements to take over the supply.

* there is no adult at home at the time and you have not been warned that you will be disconnected on or after a certain date.

* you owe money to the board for something other than fuel.

If you let the board know that you are seeking help from the local DHSS office or social services department and that they are investigating your case, your supply will not be cut off for 14 days and possibly longer. You should keep the board informed of what is happening.

High bills
If you receive an exceptionally high bill, don't assume that your meter has had a brainstorm.

* It could be that:

    ● it is based on an estimated reading
    ● your last bill was based on an estimated reading which was lower than the amount of fuel you actually used; so this bill is making up for that one
    ● the weather has been very cold and you have used more fuel
    ● you have bought a new appliance which is using extra fuel
    ● you have been at home more than usual
    ● there is a new baby or a sick or elderly person in the house and you are keeping the place warmer.

* If none of these explanations account for your high bill, it could be that the meter is faulty; it does happen, though it is rare. In the case of electricity you can ask the electricity board to check your meter: find out if there is a charge for this. If you are not satisfied with the board's findings, you can ask for a Department of Energy meter examiner to inspect your meter. His

examination is extremely thorough and his decision is legally binding.

If you query your gas bill, your gas region will send somebody round to make sure that your gas appliances are working correctly. If everything seems to be in order, you can ask for your meter to be sent away for independent testing and for a new meter to be fitted. If there turns out to be nothing wrong with your meter you will have to pay for this service.

* You should pay the bill, or at least part of it, while your meter is being investigated; otherwise you could be faced with a huge bill if the meter is found to be working correctly.

* If you are a private tenant and buy your electricity from your landlord, check that you are not paying too much. Each gas region and electricity board sets maximum prices that landlords can charge their tenants for fuel.

Estimated readings

If nobody is at home when the meter reader calls, you will be sent a bill based on an estimated reading. It is a good idea to check whether this is roughly accurate by reading the meter yourself. Otherwise you may be paying too much (and nobody wants to do that) or too little (in which case your next bill may be higher than you would like). If the estimated reading is 'out' by a long way, send your own meter reading to the gas region or electricity board at once and you will be sent an amended bill. The region or board will normally want to have the meter read by one of its staff at least once in every four readings.

Problems with electricity

* If you are unhappy with the way an area electricity board has handled your problem, or need advice that the area board has not been able to provide, you should contact your area electricity consultative council. There

is an AECC for each area board, but they are independent of the boards and exist to represent consumers' interests. You will find the address of your AECC on the back of your bill.

* If the council cannot resolve the problem with the board, it may refer the matter to the Electricity Council, the central body for the electricity supply industry in England and Wales. From there the case may go to the Secretary of State for Energy, though this is very rare.

* If the AECC thinks your complaint raises issues of national importance it may refer the matter to the Electricity Consumers' Council which represents the interests of consumers at a national level.

There are electricity consultative councils in Scotland, but not in Northern Ireland, where the General Consumer Council for Northern Ireland will investigate complaints which cannot be resolved with the electricity board. The Electricity Consumers' Council does not cover Scotland or Northern Ireland.

Problems with gas
The Gas Consumers' Council represents consumers' interests at a national level and has 12 regional offices which correspond to the regions of British Gas.

* If you are dissatisfied with the way the gas region has handled your complaint, or want independent advice about a problem, you should contact the Gas Consumers' Council regional office for your area: the address is on the back of your bill.

* If the regional office cannot resolve the problem it may refer the matter to the Gas Consumers' Council headquarters in London.

Neither British Gas nor the Gas Consumers' Council operate in Northern Ireland.

Coal

Unlike gas and electricity consumers, coal users can shop around for a supplier. And it is worth doing so as prices do vary.

Most reputable coal merchants belong to the Approved Coal Merchants' Scheme which has a code of practice covering the way firms deal with their customers. Members of the scheme carry a sign saying 'Authorised Coal Dealer' or 'Approved Coal Merchant' on their lorries and delivery tickets.

The most common complaints about coal are that it doesn't light or burn well, that the pieces are too small or there is too much dust.

* If you have a complaint, try to resolve it with your coal merchant.

* If he is unhelpful, contact the regional secretary of the Approved Coal Merchants Scheme for the area in which the merchant trades. The Scheme's regional panel will arrange to have the coal inspected and if they think your complaint is justified, will ask the merchant to compensate you.

* If you are unhappy with the Scheme's response, write to the Domestic Coal Consumers' Council. The council will look into your problem, and although it cannot actually order anybody to make amends – it has a small staff and limited powers – it is able to exert pressure and get things done. The council can also advise you on your legal rights against a merchant.

  The Approved Coal Merchants Scheme does not operate in Northern Ireland. If you have a complaint about coal, contact the Northern Ireland Coal Advisory Service or the Trading Standards Branch of the Department of Economic Development for Northern Ireland.

* If you have a problem with a coal burning appliance, or a query about the type of fuel a particular appliance uses, the Solid Fuel Advisory Service may be able to help.

Water

Water bills

Some water authorities bill quarterly, some twice a year
and others annually. Payment methods vary too but
you will usually be able to pay in instalments if you
wish: the different methods of payment are listed on
the back of your bill.

If you cannot pay your water bill, tell the water
authority immediately otherwise your supply may be
cut off. The water industry has agreed a code of practice
which says that your supply will not be cut off if:

- you agree upon and stick to an arrangement for paying
  what you owe by instalments
- there is a genuine dispute over the bill; but you must
  have questioned the bill as soon as you received it
- the debt is owed by a previous occupant of your home
- you tell the authority that you are applying for help
  to the DHSS office or local authority social services
  department and either of these offices asks the authority to delay turning off your supply.

Problems with water

* If you have a complaint concerning your water supply,
  you should contact the water authority – the address is
  on your bill or in the telephone directory under 'Water'
  – and give them a chance to sort the problem out.

* If you have no success, ask the authority for the address
  of your local water consumer consultative committee;
  there is one for each division of each of the ten water
  authorities in England and Wales. The committee will
  take the matter up with the water authority on your
  behalf.

In Scotland, water services are the responsibility of
regional councils. If you have a problem, contact the
water services department for your region. In Northern
Ireland, you should contact the water services depart-

ment at the Department of the Environment for Northern Ireland for the region in which you live.

Telephones

Buying and renting
You no longer *have* to rent any of your telephones from British Telecom, though you can still do so if you prefer. Alternatively you can buy your telephones outright – from either BT or another manufacturer. Any phone you buy should carry a label marked with a green circle: this shows it is approved for use with BT equipment. Steer clear of phones marked with a red triangle – buying one is not illegal, but connecting it to the BT system is.

British Telecom is responsible for maintaining the line to your phone and will repair faults on the line free of charge. Its engineers will service the telephone itself if you rent it from BT or if it is a BT phone you have bought and for which you have a maintenance contract. When you buy a phone, find out what arrangements there are for servicing it. Of course, if a fault develops soon after purchase, you should take it back to the shop: telephones are goods and you are protected by the Sale of Goods Act 1979 when things go wrong (see Chapter 3).

If you do not rent and have no maintenance contract and a fault develops, check whether this is on the line or in the equipment itself. You can do this by unplugging the problem telephone and plugging in another. If the fault disappears, there was probably something wrong with the equipment. If it doesn't, the problem probably lies with the line. During working hours you can ask the BT fault repair service to test your line from the exchange. There is no charge for this. You will find the fault repair service number in your telephone directory or code book. If you call out a BT engineer and the fault turns out to be in a telephone for which BT has no responsibility, you will have to pay a call-out charge.

☞ If your line is out of order for more than two days after being reported to the fault repair service, you should tell your local BT office (the address is on your phone bill). The amount you pay for your line rental will be reduced on your next bill.

Trouble getting through

If you get a wrong number, a crossed line, or one so faint or noisy you have to hang up, call the operator. Your account will be credited for the first call and, if the operator re-connects you, you will be charged a low operator rate which is about the same as if you had dialled direct. This does not apply to international calls where you have to pay full operator rates for all operator-connected calls.

Telephone bills

* You can stagger the payments for your telephone bill by using a monthly budget payment scheme, which works similarly to those for gas and electricity (see above), or by buying telephone stamps to put towards your bill from a post office.

* If you cannot pay your telephone bill, tell your local BT office immediately. In a case of genuine hardship, BT will allow you to pay off the bill by instalments and will not cut you off in the meantime.

* If you think your bill is inexplicably high, contact your local BT office. They will check the meter readings used to calculate the bill and look at your previous bills. They will also check the meter which records your calls at the exchange. If it turns out that the meter was wrong, your bill will be adjusted. This does sometimes happen, so if your bill is much higher than usual and there seems no reason, do query it. Within the next ten years we should be offered itemised bills listing the calls we make individually by number, date and length of call;

this should greatly reduce the number of queries about high bills.

<hr>

Problems with the telephone service
British Telecom has drawn up a code of practice in consultation with the Office of Fair Trading which covers most aspects of its dealings with consumers, including the way complaints are handled.

* As a first step, contact the local BT office at the address on your bill.

* If you are not happy with the way BT has dealt with your complaint – whether it concerns a bill or any other matter – you can seek advice from your local Post and Telecommunications Advisory Committee (PATAC) if there is one in your area – the address is at the back of your telephone directory.

* Alternatively, a Citizens' Advice Bureau, Consumer Advice Centre or the trading standards or consumer protection department at your local council offices may be able to help.

* If you still have no success or if there is no PATAC in your area, write to the secretary of the Advisory Committee on Telecommunications for your part of the UK – again, the address is at the back of the telephone directory. These national committees work closely with the Office of Telecommunications (OFTEL), a government body which has a duty to investigate consumers' complaints. You can, if you like, contact OFTEL direct.

* If this brings no solution and you think British Telecom owes you money, you will have to decide whether to go to arbitration or to court (see Chapter 13). The arbitration scheme used by BT deals with claims up to £1,000.

The Post
The Post Office has drawn up a Code of Practice for

Postal Services in consultation with the OFT and the Post Office Users' National Council, which covers most aspects of its dealing with consumers. Copies should be available at post offices.

Compensation for losses

* The Post Office will pay a limited amount of compensation – at present up to £20 – for letters or parcels which are lost or damaged while being sent by ordinary post.

  ● If you send something which has a small monetary value, you should get a **certificate of posting** from the counter clerk at the time of posting. Otherwise there is no proof that the package was sent and you may have difficulty in obtaining compensation.
  ● Using **recorded delivery** provides you with proof of posting and means that the article will not be delivered unless it is signed for at its destination. But compensation rates are the same as for ordinary posting. And the Post Office will not pay compensation for jewellery or money sent by either ordinary or recorded post.

* If you want to send a letter containing money or valuables, you should use the **registered letter service.** The cost of this depends on the level of compensation cover you want. If your package does get lost you will only be paid the value of the goods you have sent.

* If you send a valuable parcel you should use the **compensation fee parcel service.** The fees again depend on the level of compensation you want.

* If you want to be told when something you have sent has been delivered, you should ask for **advice of delivery**. It goes without saying that if you are sending important documents by post, you should always take a photocopy first.

* You are not normally entitled to claim compensation

merely because something is delayed in the post. However, if you take out **consequential loss insurance** when you send something by registered post, you can claim compensation for any extra financial loss you suffer as a result of its being damaged, delayed or lost.

* There are different arrangements for overseas letters and parcels and you should ask about these at the post office.

Problems with the post

* If a letter or parcel is lost or damaged in the post, you should ask at a post office for form P58 'Enquiry about a missing or damaged letter or parcel', complete it and hand it in. Do this as soon as you become aware of the loss or damage.

  At the time of writing, the Post Office is being reorganised. The old Head Postmaster who was responsible for all aspects of the service in his area will cease to exist. Instead, the Post Office is being divided up into separate businesses covering letters, parcels and counter service, with a district manager for each business. There are expected to be enquiry points at main post offices and sorting offices to which consumers can take their complaints. It is hoped that this reorganisation will speed up the way complaints are dealt with.

* If you are unhappy with the way the Post Office has handled your complaint, seek advice from your local PATAC (see above, page 134), or from a Citizens' Advice Bureau, Consumer Advice Centre or the trading standards or consumer protection department of your local council.

* If you still have no success or there is no PATAC in your area, contact the Post Office Users' Council for your part of the UK – the address is at the back of the Code of Practice or obtainable from the Post Office

Users' National Council. These councils are independent bodies set up to represent consumers' interests
and investigate complaints.

* If you think you are entitled to compensation from the
Post Office and still cannot resolve the problem, you
will have to decide whether to go to court or to arbitration (see Chapter 13).

8

Holidays and Leisure

Booking a fortnight in Benidorm, a weekend in Blackpool or just a table in your favourite restaurant is not like buying a carpet or ordering a new kitchen. For one thing, you cannot see exactly what you're getting. Even if you subject yourself to watching the interminable slides of the Smiths who stayed at the same hotel last year, you cannot be certain that you will get quite the same holiday. And even if you did, you might not enjoy it as much. For when you pay for something like a holiday or a meal in a restaurant, you are buying more than the surroundings, the decor, the service and the food. You are buying pleasure – and the problem is that your idea of paradise may be somebody else's purgatory. This fact can make people timid about complaining because they fear that they will be thought unreasonable. But if you stay silent, you cannot expect anybody to know you are dissatisfied and standards will never improve.

Restaurants

Booking a table

* If you haven't booked a table, a restaurant does not have to let you in, even if you can see it has room.

Unlike hotels, restaurants can refuse to serve you without giving a reason, as long as it is not on the grounds of your sex, colour, race or ethnic origin.

* Even if you have booked a table, a restaurant can refuse to admit you if you are drunk as a lord, behaving badly or unsuitably dressed.

* If you book a table and don't turn up or arrive very late, the owner is entitled to ask for compensation for the business he has lost – if he can trace you, that is.

* If, on the other hand, you appear in good time to be told that there will not be a table free for at least an hour, or not at all, you would be entitled to compensation for breach of contract. In theory, you could claim your expenses in travelling to the restaurant and something for the inconvenience caused. A more practical course than legal action might be to protest your disappointment noisily in the restaurant in the hope that the manager makes some compensatory offer to you in return for your swift departure from his premises.

Alec Smart took his wife and two friends to a city-centre restaurant which offered a 'pre-theatre dinner'. He booked the table for an hour and a half before the start of the show and made it clear that they would have to leave by 8.15 pm. The restaurant was full when they arrived and they had to wait 20 minutes before sitting down to eat. The service was appallingly slow and at 8 pm – when they had still not been served with their main courses – the party left. Alec paid the cost of the starters but nothing else. The restaurant took him to court, claiming the cost of the main courses – which they said had had to be thrown away – and the wine. Alec counterclaimed for the inconvenience caused. The registrar rejected the restaurant's claim and awarded Alec the compensation he had sought.

Prices

Gone are the days when you had to guess how much a restaurant meal would cost from the type of cars parked outside. By law, restaurants must display a selection of items from their menu, with prices, in a place where you can see this before you sit down to eat – usually outside the door. These prices must include VAT, and if there is a minimum charge or obligatory service charge this must be made clear: if there is no mention of these charges, you do not have to pay them.

Awful meal, appalling service?

If you are unhappy about some aspect of your meal, complain there and then. The staff may be able to put the matter right and if they can't they will be less surprised if you protest at bill-paying time. Remember, a bad meal isn't just one that is burned, takes two hours to arrive or makes you ill. It could be stone cold, badly cooked, tasteless or tough.

You are entitled to a meal and service of a reasonable standard.

* If you think your meal was below the standard you are entitled to expect for the price, you can claim compensation for breach of contract. Deduct what you think is a reasonable amount from the bill and leave your name and address. It is up to the restaurant to sue you for the rest.

* If the service was slow, rushed or simply careless, don't tip. If there is an obligatory service charge on the menu, pay it only if the service was good. If it was not, refuse to pay some or all of the service charge.

In situations like this you can ignore threats to call the police. Unless you are causing a breach of the peace or you enter the restaurant with no intention of paying for the meal – leaving your name and address and waving a walletful of credit cards should demonstrate that this is not the case – you have committed no offence and the police will not be interested.

* Should two well-built restaurant staff suddenly appear as if from nowhere in order to persuade you to change your mind, you could pay up but write 'paid under protest' across the bill. Then write a letter to the restaurant owner or manager describing what went wrong and explaining what you want him to do. Keep a copy of the letter.

* If this does not bring a satisfactory solution, you will have to consider suing the restaurant to get your money back (see Chapter 13). If you intend doing this, take statements from other members of your party and ask whether they would be prepared to act as witnesses.

* If you think something you ate in a restaurant has made you ill, tell the environmental health officer for the local authority in that area. He will investigate. You may be able to sue the restaurant for the suffering – and perhaps loss of earnings – caused. A successful prosecution by the environmental health department would be likely to help your case.

Holidays
How long do you spend planning your holiday and researching the different options? A few hours probably. A few evenings at most. Considering how much holidays cost and how much we look forward to them, most of us do pitifully little homework beforehand. A little extra time invested before you book can mean the difference between a fortnight to remember and one you'd rather forget.

Hotels in Britain

CHOOSING A HOTEL
Finding a hotel which matches up to its brochure is not always easy. If possible, go by the recommendation of a friend with similar tastes to yours. Consult some hotel guides – most libraries have a selection in the reference section. If you cross-refer between a few guides you

will get a fuller picture of what the place is really like. Remember that in some guides the hotels *pay* to be included while in others they are inspected and judged anonymously. In some guides the classifications are based on the facilities offered – the proportion of rooms with en suite bathrooms, the level of room service and so on – while in others they are based on the inspector's personal taste.

When you have made a shortlist, ask for a brochure and tariff from each. Before you book find out:

- what your stay will cost including VAT and service charges

- what meals are included in the price

- what type of room you will have with what facilities

- what other facilities the hotel offers – for children perhaps

- what time meals are served, if this matters to you

- whether the hotel is quiet or noisy, if this matters to you.

If there is anything you want to know, ring the hotel. You can tell a good deal from the attitude of the staff over the phone.

MAKING A BOOKING

* The hotel industry has agreed a voluntary code of booking practice with the Department of Trade and Industry which covers all hotels, guest houses and similar establishments with more than three bedrooms. Its aim is to ensure that you know before you book what you will pay and what you will get for your money. The code says that you should be told in writing before you book:

  - what the total charge for your room will be. This

will be broken down into the charge per person or
per room, either per night or per week depending
on the booking. VAT and any obligatory service
charge will be included
- whether the charge includes a bath or shower and
  WC
- what meals are included in the price
- if there is an extra charge for any of the advertised
  hotel facilities
- if the accommodation is in an annexe and whether
  this differs in comfort from the main hotel.

* If you turn up at a hotel at a reasonable hour without a
  booking you must be offered a room unless the place is
  full, or you are drunk or badly dressed, behaving badly
  or of bad character. This rule doesn't apply to guest
  houses, boarding houses or bed and breakfasts, which
  can turn visitors away for any reason except on the
  grounds of their sex, race, colour or ethnic origin.

* Hotels are entitled to ask for a deposit when you book.
  If you do not turn up, the proprietor can keep this and –
  if he cannot fill your room – claim some money from
  you for his lost profit. (Just how much depends on the
  circumstances: the courts have been known to allow up
  to two-thirds of the full-board charge.) If the proprietor
  manages to fill your room – and he must make an effort
  to do so – he will not be able to claim from you because
  he will not have suffered any loss.

* If you have booked a room somewhere and turn up to
  find the place is full, you could claim compensation for
  your travelling expenses and any other costs you have
  incurred as a result of the hotel's breach of contract.

Simon Simple took a motoring holiday in England
and booked up a number of hotels on his route.
After staying a night in the first, he decided it was
so pleasant that he would remain another three
days, instead of moving on. He did not bother to
notify the hotel he had booked for the next stage

of his holiday. When he returned home, a letter awaited him from the second hotel, explaining that they had been unable to let his room for the first night of his booking and were therefore claiming from him the profit they had lost. Simon ignored this letter, but paid up on the advice of a solicitor friend after receiving another letter from the hotel threatening court proceedings for breach of contract.

CHARGES

A hotel must display its charges at the door or at reception. These must include VAT. The prices for single and double rooms must be given.

YOUR BELONGINGS

When you stay at a hotel, the proprietor is responsible for any loss or damage to your belongings (except your car), unless you yourself were to blame. The proprietor cannot wriggle out of his responsibility completely, but he can limit his liability to £50 per item, or £100 in all, if he displays a notice to this effect. If there is no notice, or if the damage is caused by the negligence of hotel staff, these limits do not apply.

IF YOU HAVE A COMPLAINT

* If the bed is as full of lumps as yesterday's porridge, the bathroom the size of a small broom cupboard and the previous occupant's hairs are all over the dressing table, ask to see the manager. Outline your complaint calmly and say what you would like done about it. The matter may be simple to resolve. If not, or if the problem is that the hotel's facilities do not match those described in its brochure, you are entitled to compensation for breach of contract or misrepresentation. Deduct what you think is a reasonable amount from the bill and leave your name and address. If the hotel wants more, it will sue. Alternatively, pay the bill, but write 'paid under protest' across it. When you get home,

write to the hotel proprietor or to the head office if it is part of a chain.

* If this does not resolve matters, write to the Membership Department of the British Hotels, Restaurants and Caterers Association, which will investigate complaints against its 16,000 members.

* If you are still not satisfied, you will have to consider legal action (see Chapter 13).

Self-catering holidays
This section is intended mainly for people booking self-catering holidays in the UK, but some of the guidelines apply equally to foreign holidays.

At its best a self-catering holiday gives you the comforts of home without the restrictions and the cost of a hotel. At its worst it means you pay good money to stay in a place which has none of the comforts of your home and none of the service of a hotel. You are less likely to find that the chocolate box, roses-round-the-door dream cottage you thought you booked is actually a two-up-two-down in a terrace on an arterial road if you follow the 'buy-laws':

☞ Choose a place featured in a reliable guide to self-catering accommodation. Some organisations, including the AA and local tourist boards, inspect the properties they list. But remember that the classification in some guides is based on the facilities offered while in others it is based on the inspectors' personal preferences.

☞ Book through a company which specialises in letting holiday homes. As these generally rely on recommendation, they should try to please and take notice of complaints. Pick a company which is well-established and preferably inspects all the properties it offers. If it has a brochure with a description and photograph of each holiday home, so much the better.

☞   Ask every question you can think of before you book –
and then a few more – from whether there is mains
drainage to what the view is like. And confirm the
information you are given in writing. In particular find
out about:

- the number and sizes of the rooms
- the number and location of the beds – this is important: 'sleeps 8' can mean four in beds and the
  rest in put-you-ups in the living-room
- how electricity and gas are paid for: you don't want
  to spend the first night in darkness because you
  didn't bring coins for the meter
- what arrangements there are for cleaning the place
  between lets
- whether the place is safe for children: the owners
  may forget to mention that 'magnificent views'
  means there's a sheer 40 foot drop to the beach at
  the bottom of the garden
- how many dining chairs and armchairs there are:
  otherwise you could find yourself playing musical
  chairs at mealtimes, or drawing lots for the sofa
- where the nearest shops, beach, restaurants and
  telephone are and whether the location is quiet or
  noisy, if this is important to you.

☞   Ask to talk to people who have rented the place before.
This may be easier, and more important, when you are
renting privately than through an agency.

IF YOU HAVE A COMPLAINT

*   If you are unhappy about your accommodation, contact
the landlord or the company through which you booked
and give them a chance to sort the problem out while you
are on holiday.

*   If you have no success, visit your nearest Tourist
Information Office. If the property is one they have
approved, their officers will mediate for you. If it is not,
they will give you advice on what you can do.

* If you found the place through a guide, write and tell the compilers of your problems: this won't help you but it may prevent others having an unhappy holiday.

* You may be entitled to compensation for breach of contract if the place falls short of what you could reasonably have expected or for misrepresentation if a false statement of fact helped persuade you to choose the holiday. If you cannot sort the matter out with the landlord or the agency, you will have to consider whether to take legal action (see Chapter 13).

Timesharing

Many people enjoy the freedom of self-catering but resent paying out money each year for holiday homes which will never be theirs. For those who cannot afford a second home, timesharing is one solution.

For a lump sum, you buy a specified week or weeks each year at a particular development. The idea is sold as a passport to inflation-free holidaymaking for the rest of your life and a means of buying a luxury second home at a fraction of its real value. And if all goes well, it can be both these things. However, it is essential to go into timesharing with your eyes wide open; otherwise it can turn out to be an expensive disaster. So once again, follow the 'buy-laws':

☞ Choose your accommodation, resort, country and climate very carefully. Never buy a timeshare without seeing the property first, if possible at the time of the year you intend to purchase. Some companies arrange inspection flights for potential buyers of foreign time-shares.

☞ If the development is not complete, find out what guarantees buyers have that the promised facilities will materialise. You may be safer with a mature scheme where you can see how things are working out.

☞ Ask to talk to some people who have already bought timeshares on the development.

☞ Compare as many schemes as possible before you choose. High-pressure sales techniques are used by some companies to sell timesharing. Don't let yourself be salestalked into a hasty purchase or you may end up – literally – repenting at leisure.

☞ Study the management contract carefully and make sure you have some protection against soaring maintenance charges. There should also be a clause which allows timesharers to sack the management company if a majority is unhappy with the way the development is run.

☞ Make sure your home and its contents are properly insured.

☞ Ask whether you can exchange your week for time at a different resort: people do tend to get bored after a few holidays in the same place. There are organisations which will arrange exchanges for you; but you will be expected to swap like for like – so any timesharer hoping to trade a winter week in his studio flat in Cornwall for a beachside villa in Portugal in July is in for a disappointment.

☞ Find out if you can let, bequeath or sell your timeshare.

☞ Don't regard a timeshare as an investment. Selling it may not be easy, especially if the development is unfinished and you are competing with the developer who has a wider range of homes and times to sell.

You will give yourself extra protection if you:

● buy from a big name company rather than a small-time developer
● buy from a company which belongs to an association that vets its members and has a code of practice
● consult a solicitor before you sign.

Package holidays

BEFORE YOU BOOK

How do you choose your holiday from the brochures – with a pin, by intuition, from the photograph and the description? There will always be some people who are unhappy with their holiday – some punters seem strangely determined to have a bad time while others are just plain unlucky. But the more you can discover about your destination in advance, the less likely you are to be disappointed.

* The first rule is to get as many brochures as you can and compare them. Always assume that the most pessimistic description, photograph and star-rating is accurate – a sad fact but generally true. If one brochure calls the beach 'sandy and pebbly' while another describes it as just 'pebbly', you can assume that you will have to start digging towards Australia before you come across any sand. Brochure descriptions are more reliable than they were – I once stayed in an Italian hotel billed as a 'stone's throw from the sea' which turned out to be up in the hills seven miles from the coast – but you should still read between the lines.

* Once you have chosen your resort, work out when you want to travel (the time of day and of year), how much you want to spend and what kind of hotel you want. Then make a list of the possible alternatives and their total cost.

* If there are wide differences in price between holidays in the same hotel, find out why. It may be that one tour operator offers a room with a sea view as standard while another flies you out at 4 am and then gives you a room overlooking the dustbins.

* Bear in mind the charges for children when you calculate the total cost. If one company offers a particularly good deal for the under-5s it may be cheaper to book with them than with another operator whose basic price is lower.

* Ask friends which tour operators they would recommend and which they would not use again. Surveys by *Which?* have shown that some operators have a much better record of customer satisfaction than others.

* When you have narrowed down your choice to a few hotels, visit the travel agent. If you are lucky and he has sent many customers to that resort before – or even been there himself – he may be able to give you some useful background information. However, you are equally likely to find that the travel agent knows less than you do. If you have burning questions, make him ring the tour operator and get the answers for you. If you want a more honest assessment of a resort or hotel than you suspect appears in the brochure, ask to see the *Agent's Hotel Gazetteer*, which most agents keep well out of sight under the counter. This gives a brief and unglamorised account of resort hotels.

* If there are any aspects of the holiday which are particularly important to you, ask about these before you book and confirm them in writing when you make your booking. A friend who likes to rise at midday used to eliminate anywhere that was near an early morning market, holiday camp or main road – and was woken at 6 am on the first morning of her supposedly idyllic holiday by the peel of church bells. She now confirms in writing that there are 'no known sources of loud noise' near the hotel.

THE ABTA CODE OF CONDUCT

Like many trade associations, ABTA has drawn up a code of conduct with the agreement of the Office of Fair Trading. But, unlike some, the ABTA code does seem to work. This is because ABTA has a virtual monopoly of the package tour industry and can – and does – discipline members who breach the code. It doesn't often eject members but the threat of having to survive without ABTA affiliation is enough to keep most tour operators roughly in line.

The ABTA code says that:

- Brochures should be clear, comprehensive and accurate and should enable you to work out what the holiday is going to cost, what you will get for your money and the circumstances under which the tour operator can alter the price.

- Booking conditions should not include clauses which try to allow the operator to wriggle out of his legal responsibilities to you. However, this doesn't mean you need not read the small print in the brochure: tour operators may well try to limit their responsibility for holiday problems caused by people they don't employ – like the hotelier. But if it came to the crunch in court, they would have to show that these exclusions were reasonable (see Chapter 5, pages 77–9).

- If a tour operator has to cancel or substantially alter your holiday, you must be told as soon as possible and given the choice of another holiday of the same or higher standard or a full refund. Operators must not cancel holidays after the date when the balance of the payment is due, and if they alter them substantially after that date then they must pay you some compensation. In any case they must not make major alterations less than 14 days before your departure.

- A tour operator must not impose surcharges caused by currency fluctuations less than 30 days before your departure. If he imposes any other kind of surcharge he must be able to show that this is caused by reasons beyond his control – for example, a rise in the price of fuel. Some tour operators guarantee in their brochures that you will not have to pay surcharges of more than a certain amount per person. Check before you book.

- If you arrive at your hotel to find there is no bed for you, you must be offered alternative accommodation, and if this is of a lower standard than the hotel you originally booked you must be paid some compensation.

PROTECTING YOUR MONEY
When you book a holiday, you need to be sure that you

will not lose your money – and your holiday – if the tour operator goes out of business before you leave or while you are away.

* If the tour operator is a member of the Association of British Travel Agents (ABTA) – and 90 per cent are – you are well protected by the ABTA bonding scheme. If the company goes bust before your holiday has started, you will be offered another holiday of equivalent standard or your money back. If the company collapses while you are away, you will normally be able to continue the holiday and will be brought back to the UK.

* If you book a holiday which includes a charter flight or a charter-type block booking on a scheduled flight, then you have similar protection because all tour operators involved in this kind of holiday must have an Air Travel Organiser's Licence (ATOL). This means they have paid money into a central fund which will be used to bring holidaymakers home if the company goes out of business.

* If you have booked a scheduled flight which is not part of a tour operator's charter package, then you have no protection if the airline goes bust.

* If your package holiday includes coach travel and is organised by a member of the Bus and Coach Council then you will have the protection of their bonding scheme.

* If your money is not covered by any of the schemes described above, then there are two ways you can protect it:

  ● by taking out an insurance policy which covers bankruptcy of the tour operator
  ● by paying with a credit card – but the holiday must have cost more than £100 and the payment must have been made direct to the tour operator (see Chapter 11, pages 221–3).

INSURANCE

When you book your holiday take out insurance which covers:

* the cancellation or curtailment of your holiday – owing to illness or bereavement for example. Make sure you are actually covered for the eventualities which will prevent your travelling – pregnancy, perhaps, or the illness of your business partner.

* medical expenses. Do check with your travel agent that the cover is adequate, especially if you are travelling to America.

* personal liability. This will cover you if you accidentally injure somebody or damage their property.

* your money and luggage. But don't expect the insurance company to pay out if you don't take proper care of your belongings – by leaving them unattended on a crowded beach while you take a dip, for example.

* personal accident while on holiday.

* missing the plane as a result of a public transport hold-up on the way to the airport. This will pay a certain amount towards extra expenses you incur.

If you are travelling to a European country which is a member of the Common Market you should also take with you Form E.111 – your local social security office will tell you how to get one. If you need urgent medical treatment this form will enable you to obtain it as if you were a resident of the country you are in.

BEFORE YOU GO

If the package tour industry is having a lean year and the operators cannot fill all their flights, you may find that your holiday is 'consolidated' – or as we ordinary mortals would put it, changed – so that your tour firm can send out one full plane instead of two half-empty ones.

A tour operator who belongs to ABTA must follow their code of conduct if he makes a major change to your holiday (see above). If your trip is substantially altered (and most firms define what counts as a 'substantial alteration' in their booking conditions) you have two choices: accept the change or ask for a refund. If you decide to go but are unhappy about the new arrangements, let the operator know in writing; this should strengthen your position if the holiday is a disaster and you want to claim against the operator.

Six weeks before Alec Smart was due to go on holiday, the tour operator informed him that the hotel he had booked had gone out of business and the only holiday available at a hotel of the same standard was at a different resort. Knowing that it would be impossible to get in anywhere else in mid-August, Alec accepted the proposal, but made it clear in a letter to the operator that he was unhappy about the change. As things turned out the hotel was delightful, but the resort had none of the amenities for children and adults which had particularly appealed to the Smarts when they made their original choice. On his return, Alec claimed compensation for breach of contract from the tour operator for the disappointment the family had experienced. After at first refusing, the company ultimately paid up.

As a precaution, take a photocopy of your completed booking form with you on holiday, along with a copy of the brochure entry for your hotel. These can be useful evidence if the place does not match up to expectations and you want to complain to the tour representative.

FLIGHT DELAYS
Nobody wants to spend the first 24 hours of their Mediterranean holiday in the departure lounge of an overcrowded and stuffy British airport along with hundreds of other equally disappointed would-be

travellers. Knowing this, many tour operators now offer compensation – or the option of cancelling your holiday – if your departure is greatly delayed. Check before you book. Otherwise take out delay compensation insurance.

If your return flight is delayed, you may also be entitled to compensation, depending on the cause. If the airline is to blame, because the flight has been overbooked or there is a problem with the plane, you should claim from them for any inconvenience or extra expenses you have incurred.

WHEN YOU ARRIVE: AVOIDING THE RIP-OFFS

Hiring a car. Your friends will invariably tell you to wait until you arrive and go to a cut-price local firm. But if you book from home you may actually get a better deal when all the extras like insurance have been taken into account. Also, if things go wrong, you *may* have a better chance of redress than if you were trying to argue your case with the locals. Before you drive away, make sure you have all the right documents and the insurance cover you need. And examine the car for damage: you don't want to pay for the last hirer's close encounter with a tree.

Taxis. Try to avoid taxis without a meter. Always ask how much the journey is going to cost before you step inside.

At the hotel. Pay for everything as you go along. That way you won't be presented with a horrifying bill when you can least afford it – at the end of your stay. If you must run up a bar bill, note down everything you spend and check it against the bill at the end. Phone-calls from your room can cost several times the actual rate, so use a call-box.

Eating out. Always check your restaurant bills – a pocket calculator is a useful addition to your holiday luggage. Before you leave a tip, check that service is not included in the bill. When you pay by credit card, make

sure the bottom line of the counterfoil is filled in before
you sign.

HOW TO COMPLAIN ABOUT YOUR HOLIDAY

If your hotel turns out to be a far cry from its description
in the brochure, the swimming pool is the size of a
fishpond, the 'international cuisine' is soggy fish and
chips, the service is so poor it would shame Basil
Fawlty, and your room has fungus growing from the
walls – or there is no room for you at all and you have to
move somewhere else – **don't suffer in silence.** For one
thing, the problem may be easily resolved. For another,
no tour operator is going to take your claim for compensation very seriously if you did not even bother to
tell the rep that you were dissatisfied. On the other
hand there is no point in complaining if it pours with
rain, or there's a coach driver's strike and you cannot do
any day trips, or your one-star hotel isn't as comfortable as the three-star one next door. On holiday as
everywhere else, you get what you pay for.

* If you think you have real cause for complaint, the first
thing you should do is to tell the rep and ask him to sort
the problem out. This may be the time to produce the
booking form and brochure entry as 'evidence'.

* If you have no success within a day, start making a fuss
before your holiday ticks away. Telegram the managing
director of the tour operator. Then start collecting
evidence. If possible, take photographs of the cause of
your complaint – the six-lane highway you have to
cross before you can get to the beach from your 'sea-
front' hotel, the bank of lethal-looking rocks (unmen-
tioned in the brochure) which lie between you and the
'warm blue waters of the Mediterranean'. If you needed
medical treatment because the hotel meals gave you
food poisoning, get a medical certificate to prove it.
Take written statements from others to back up your
claim. The more of you who are dissatisfied, the more
likely you are to get a sympathetic hearing.

* When you get home, write immediately to the managing

director of the tour operator setting out your complaint clearly, concisely and without resorting to emotional language or threats. Enclose any photographs or written evidence you have and keep copies of everything you send. Remember to include:

- your travel dates, the time and place of your departure and arrival
- the name of your hotel and the resort
- your booking reference number and the name in which the holiday was booked
- the nature of your complaint and what you did about it while on holiday.

Explain that in your view the company is in breach of contract and that you are therefore seeking compensation. Say how much money you want. It could include any extra expenses you've incurred – such as bus fares into town because your hotel was overbooked and you were transferred to one two miles out of the resort – plus compensation for breach of contract, disappointment and inconvenience. If a false statement in the brochure helped persuade you to book that holiday, you may have a claim for misrepresentation. The size of your claim will depend on how inferior the holiday you got was to the one you were entitled to expect for your money. Ask for more than you will be prepared to accept – though don't make the amount ridiculous or you may not be taken seriously.

The company is quite likely to disclaim responsibility for your problems and to offer you no compensation at all or very little. **Do not be deterred.** If they blame the hotelier and point to the clause in their booking conditions which says they do not accept liability for the actions of people not employed by them, take no notice. A court would probably take the view that it was not reasonable for a package tour operator to try to duck responsibility for a lousy hotel.

---

* If you are not satisfied with the tour operator's response, write to him again saying why, and – if he is a member of ABTA – write to the Association's Consumer Affairs Department enclosing photocopies of your correspondence. ABTA operates a free conciliation service and will mediate between you and the tour operator. A conciliation team will investigate your complaint and may recommend that you should be paid compensation. But it cannot compel the operator to pay up.

* If you paid for a holiday costing more than £100 (and not many holidays cost less) by credit card, the card company is equally liable if things go wrong. So if you get no satisfaction from the tour operator, contact the card company (see Chapter 12, pages 221–3).

* If you are still dissatisfied, you must consider whether to take your case to court or arbitration (see Chapter 13). If you have a good case, the more determined you are and the longer you pursue your claim, the more money you are likely to get. Of the cases that go to arbitration, the vast majority are judged in favour of the customer, with the average holidaymaker getting between a third and half of the amount he originally claimed.

Alec Smart and his family booked a package holiday at a luxury Mediterranean hotel. The holiday was a disappointment from start to finish. The bedrooms were small and sparsely furnished – nothing like those in the brochure – and the food in the 'international restaurant' was almost inedible. The children's entertainer had left the week before and the 'buffet-style lunch by the pool' only materialised on two out of the 14 days. Alec complained to the tour operator's rep who made sympathetic noises but could do nothing. When he returned home he wrote to the tour operator claiming that the company had breached its contract in not providing the holiday the family were entitled to expect. He asked them to refund half the cost of the holiday. At first the company blamed the hotel and refused to pay anything. Finally they offered to repay Alec a quarter of what the holiday cost. He accepted.

* If a tour operator makes a statement in his brochure knowing that it is false, he is in breach of the Trade Descriptions Act 1968. This would be the case if a hotel turned out to be two miles rather than the promised two minutes from the sea, or if the brochure advertised a hairdressing salon when none had ever existed. If this is the case, tell the trading standards or consumer protection department at your local council offices. Courts have power to award compensation to anybody who has suffered as a result of a false trade description. Even if you do not obtain compensation this way, a successful prosecution would strengthen your own case for breach of contract or misrepresentation.

Air Travel

The cost of flying
When booking an airline ticket, the golden rule is not to pay more than you need. The more flexibility you demand about when you fly, the more you will have to spend. The options include:

* a **full fare** ticket is valid for a year. You can change or cancel your booking up to the last minute or switch to a different airline on the same route.

* **Advanced Passenger Excursion Fares (APEX)** usually cost between half and two-thirds of the normal economy fare. They must be paid for in advance and can be used only for the named flight. There is a hefty charge for changes or cancellations.

* Other **budget fares** for scheduled flights may work out cheaper than APEX. Ask your travel agent.

* **Charter flights** are even cheaper than discounted scheduled flight fares but may have even more restrictions. They are return only and the choice of dates and the length of stay is restricted. If you cancel you lose your money.

* **Bucket shops** advertise in magazines and newspapers. They take the tickets the airlines cannot sell and pass them on to the public at huge discounts. There are dangers, however. The ticket might turn out to be invalid and the agent may have disappeared. Protect yourself by checking with the airline that your flight actually exists and that you have a seat. Confirm your return flight as soon as you reach your destination. And don't pay more than a small deposit until the ticket is in your hand.

When you book a cheap flight, make sure that the tour operator holds an Air Travel Organiser's Licence (ATOL) issued by the Civil Aviation Authority or is an agent for an ATOL holder. Otherwise you will lose your money if the company goes bust. Check the booking conditions carefully and take out insurance in case you have to cancel your flight. Finally, if you are taking children along, work out the total costs of different types of fare: the reductions for children vary greatly.

Delays
Normally, airlines are not obliged to pay compensation for delays. However, most will provide meals and accommodation if necessary. If they don't, get together with others on the flight and protest to an airline representative. If you are claiming compensation, you will have to prove that the delay was caused by the airline's negligence.

Overbooking
Airlines often overbook flights because they know that some passengers won't turn up. Sometimes, of course, they get their sums wrong, there is not enough room on the plane for everybody who shows up and some passengers have to be 'bumped' onto a different flight. If this happens to you, and you are delayed, you may be entitled to compensation, depending on the length of the delay. Most scheduled airlines participate in an

agreed compensation scheme and you should ask for a form to apply for **denied boarding compensation.**

Lost luggage

    Passenger: 'I would like a ticket to Paris, but I want my luggage to go to Bombay.'

    Airline official: 'I'm sorry, sir, that's impossible.'

    Passssenger: 'Why? You managed it last time.'

If you arrive at your destination but your luggage does not, report it immediately to the airline's representative at the airport: it may still be on the plane. If not, ask for the Lost and Found office and give your name and address and other relevant information. Get a note from the office to show that you have reported the loss.

If your luggage is damaged or something is missing, report it as soon as you notice, but in any case within seven days. However, the amount airlines pay for lost or damaged baggage is paltry, so if you have insurance, you would do better to claim under your policy.

To reduce the risk of lost or damaged baggage:

---

* Put your name and a contact address on the **outside** of the bag.

---

* Don't overpack your suitcase. If it looks like a melon about to burst, it probably will under pressure in the hold of an aircraft.

---

* Lock your case and put a strap round it. This also makes it easier to identify your luggage on the conveyor belt.

---

* Don't buy a case with protruding wheels or straps: they are liable to be damaged.

Complaining about air travel

---

* If you have a complaint, try to sort the problem out on the spot by talking to somebody in authority.

* If you have no success, note down the name and position of the person to whom you spoke. Write to the customer relations department of the airline including details of the destination, date, time and number of your flight. If possible, send copies of your tickets and receipts for any expenses you have incurred. Outline your complaint clearly and concisely and say what action you took at the time, what response you had to your problem and what compensation you are seeking.

* If you do not get a satisfactory response, contact the Air Transport Users' Committee (AUC) who may take up the complaint on your behalf.

* If you get nowhere, you will have to consider whether to take legal action (see Chapter 13).

The AUC publish a free booklet, *Flight Plan*, which gives useful tips on virtually every aspect of air travel.

9

You and your Car

What to Buy

Your home apart, a car is probably the most expensive item you will ever buy. In one sense a car is like any other consumer durable and the same kind of rules apply when choosing one. However, like the clothes you wear, a car is an expression of your own personality and lifestyle and these factors too will influence your choice. What follows is intended to help you make the right decision when you buy a car and to prevent you picking one just because it happens to have an electric ashtray, blue suede seats and gold-plated hubcaps.

The list of points to consider before you buy a new car is almost endless. Here are the main ones:

☞ Does it have all the features you want in terms of design, comfort and performance? Make a list of those that are important to you — based on cars you've owned or driven in the past – and **remember the list when you're actually comparing and test driving cars.**

☞ Is it within your price range and is it good value for money? Don't let yourself be talked into paying for 'extras' you don't really need.

☞   How do others rate that model? If you know anybody who owns one, ask their opinion. Consult the car magazines.

☞   Is it pleasant to drive? A test drive is an essential, though not infallible, part of assessing a car. Check comfort, controls, visibility, steering and how the car drives and parks.

☞   What are the running costs? Bear in mind its fuel consumption (and compare the figure given in the sales literature with the results of road tests carried out by the car magazines); the cost and frequency of servicing; the price of spare parts; and its insurance rating.

☞   Is there a warranty and what does it cover?

☞   Can you get the car serviced easily and by a garage you trust? If it takes you two hours and four changes on the bus to get back from your nearest franchised dealer, who has an appalling reputation anyway, you may be wise to consider another make.

Where to Buy

New cars
Once you've chosen the car you want, don't just meander into your local showroom to see if they can get you one in the colour you like. Shop around for the best deal. When you discuss this with each dealer, bear in mind:

• the on-the-road price of the new model, not just the basic list price
• the price the dealer is offering for your present car.

If the dealer who makes you the best offer is not the one you'd ideally like to buy from, give the showroom you prefer an opportunity to match the better deal.

There is one point worth remembering if you buy your car away from home. Although any dealer franchised for that make will service it for you under warranty, a dealer who did not actually sell you the car in the first place may feel less inclined to be helpful in matters such as lending you a hire car if yours is off the road – when you are not covered by the warranty but where the dealer can use his discretion. A dealer who has not only sold you one car, but hopes to sell you another in a few years time, may be more obliging.

You can sometimes save quite large sums of money by buying your car abroad. You can either do this yourself or find a company to do it for you. Obviously, using a company involves you in less hassle but you should make sure you are dealing with a reputable firm – a number of consumers have lost money this way. Above all, don't pay the full cost of the car until you've taken delivery, and make sure the car you will get meets British standards and specifications. The Consumers' Association has produced a step-by-step guide to buying abroad called *ACTION KIT – Importing a Car*.

Used cars

FROM A GARAGE

If price is your only concern, you will probably do better buying and selling privately than through a garage. But the law gives you much better protection when things go wrong if you have bought from a trader (see below, pages 176–7), and buying privately can sometimes turn out to be a false economy. On the other hand, a rogue trader can land you in equally deep water: your legal rights are worth little if he has sold you a lemon and then shut up shop. Choosing the right garage is, if anything, even more important than choosing the right car.

You are less likely to be taken for a ride if you buy from a dealer who belongs to a trade association that backs the Code of Practice for the Motor Industry, agreed with the Office of Fair Trading (see page 181). Research by the OFT shows that customers who buy from code members are more likely to be satisfied with their used car than those who buy from dealers who do not subscribe to the code. There are also fewer prosecutions of trade association members for 'clocking' – altering the car's mileage reading – than among non-code dealers.

Go for a garage which is well established and where the sales staff are friendly and helpful. If they adopt a take-it-or-leave-it attitude, leave *them* alone. At the other end of the sales spectrum, beware of high-pressure techniques. The salesman should be willing to tell you about the car's faults as well as its plus points. Code members are supposed to carry out a detailed pre-sales inspection and to display a checklist of the results inside the car. However, many dealers do not automatically show buyers the checklist because they believe that declaring the car's faults may drive their potential customers into the forecourt of the dealer down the road who is less honest. It is worth asking if there is a checklist you can inspect.

Don't automatically choose the dealer who gives you the best price for your old car. Many's the customer who's bought the wrong car because the car he should have bought was being sold by a garage which offered him less in part-exchange. Choose the car you want first, then ask about trade-in deals.

Find out what warranty the garage offers, if any, on its used cars and study the terms carefully (see below, page 173).

If you can build up a relationship with a local garage over a number of years, you will find in time that this is worth its weight in warranties. A dealer who knows that you will return to him each time you change your car is not going to kill the golden goose by selling you a dud. And some dealers make valuable concessions to their regular customers, like letting them borrow a car for an afternoon so they can try before they buy.

AT AN AUCTION

As we have seen (Chapter 3, page 53), buying anything at auction can be a risky business unless you know what you are doing because the law gives you relatively little protection. Considering how much money you are spending, you do not get much time to examine the goods at a car auction and there is the added danger that you will be carried away by the atmosphere and the bidding and end up with a bad buy. So, unless you are pretty knowledgeable, buying at auction is not generally a good idea. If you are considering buying this way:

* Visit the auction of your choice a few times first to see how it works.

* Read the conditions of sale so that you know what your rights are.

* If you know nothing about cars, take somebody along with you who does.

* Take note of what the auctioneer does – and does not – say about the car in which you are interested.

* Only buy a car which is sold 'with warranty'. The warranty in this case means that the auctioneer will give the seller's description of the condition of the car. If you discover a major undisclosed defect, you have a certain length of time – anything from one hour to one day depending on the auction – in which to register a complaint. If the car is sold without a warranty or 'as seen with all faults', there is nothing you can do if you end up with a lemon.

* Take a good look at the car before the sale: defects you can see are not usually covered by the warranty.

Some car auctions belong to the Society of Motor Auctions, which operates a code of practice (not backed by the OFT) and a conciliation procedure for disputes.

Buying privately
Once again, if things go wrong, the protection you have from the law is very limited. Take somebody else along when you go to look at the car. At the very least, he could be a useful witness if the seller turns out to have been lying through his teeth. And if he knows something about cars, so much the better. Ask lots of

questions (see below, page 169) and write down the answers. Don't buy at night or in the rain. Inspect the car carefully and insist on going for a test drive (making sure that you have adequate insurance first). If the owner won't let you take the wheel, be wary – he may have something to hide.

THE 'PRIVATE DEALER'

Because you have so few rights when you buy privately, rogue dealers often masquerade as private individuals. A survey carried out in Oxfordshire suggested that there were 100 such traders operating in that county alone, with a turnover of £2.5 million.

The 'private' dealer has an armoury of tricks to prevent detection, including using a network of telephone numbers in advertisements, taking calls in public phoneboxes and waiting for you in the street when you come to look at the car. Smell a rat if:

- you see lots of 'small ads' wth the same telephone number
- you enquire about the car and a voice asks 'Which car?'
- there seem to be a few untaxed cars parked near the one you are looking at.

It is illegal for a trader to advertise in a way which suggests he is a private seller. So if you suspect somebody of trying to do this, tell your local trading standards or consumer protection department. And stay away from the car: honest brokers don't sell this way.

Used Cars: How Not to Get Taken for a Ride

Ask any consumer adviser to tell you what people complain about most and the chances are he will put secondhand cars near the top of the list. Research by the Office of Fair Trading showed that, while the vast majority of people were satisfied with the used car they bought, one in five discovered a fault in their new vehicle which they thought the dealer should have pointed out. By definition, a used car is not going to be perfect. The important thing is that you should know in advance exactly what, if anything, is wrong with it. You may choose a vehicle knowing that it has given ten years loyal service to a car rental firm: that is your decision. But you should not be deceived into thinking it has had one lady owner who only used it to go to and from church each Sunday.

I have already pointed out the importance of *where* you buy. But there are other steps you can take to protect yourself when you choose. For example, always ask about the car's age, mileage, history and whether it has ever been involved in a serious accident. Try to find out about its service history, too.

Mileage

Although you will obviously want to know the mileage of any car in which you are interested, don't take too much notice of what the odometer says. For one thing, the reading may not be accurate. For another, mileage alone does not give a true indication of the condition of a car. The *way* it has been driven is equally important.

The 'clocking' of used cars – that is, winding back the odometer so it gives a false mileage reading – is estimated to cost consumers as much as £100 million a year in overpayments. Some experts reckon that a car loses £30 in value for every 1,000 miles it has done above the average 12,000 a year, so it is obviously in the interests of unscrupulous traders to doctor the mileage reading – especially when the fines imposed by the courts for this offence are relatively small in comparison with the profits that can be made. In one case, a trader bought a car for £2,100 at auction with 78,000 miles on the clock and sold it for £4,500 with 38,000 miles. He was fined £500 for breaching the Trade Descriptions Act.

Unless you are absolutely confident that the mileage reading is correct – if the garage can show you a complete service history for example – take the stated mileage with a pinch of salt and pay close attention to the overall condition of the car.

A garage which sells a car with a false odometer reading is committing an offence under the Trade Descriptions Act 1968 (unless it can prove one of the defences). If the garage is not certain whether the odometer reading is correct, or knows that it is wrong, it should display a disclaimer notice saying something like 'we do not guarantee the accuracy of the recorded mileage' or 'the recorded mileage is incorrect'. This notice should by law be clear and attached next to or on top of the odometer. The trouble is that in practice you may still be influenced by the actual reading and some unscrupulous garages may even encourage you to disregard the disclaimer by saying they 'have' to use it even though the reading is accurate (though they are probably committing an offence if they do this). If you see a disclaimer, you should take no notice of the odometer reading. If you don't, ask the garage what steps it has taken to check the mileage. If the odometer has been put back to nought, ask why. If there isn't an obvious explanation – like a new engine – it could mean the car has done a very high mileage.

Simon Simple bought a five-year-old car with only 25,000 miles on the clock. A few weeks later, at a party, he met the previous owner who told him the car had actually done 60,000 miles. Simon returned to the garage, which was uncooperative. So he contacted the trading standards department at his local council offices. They successfully prosecuted the trader for a breach of the Trade Descriptions Act. Simon then sued the garage under the Sale of Goods Act 1979, because the car was not 'as described'. He claimed the difference between what he paid for it and what he would have paid had he known its true mileage. He won his case.

Checking over the car

In an ideal world every buyer of a secondhand car would check the vehicle over from top to bottom – or get somebody else to do it for him – before he parted with his cash. The many checks you can and should make before you buy a used car are too numerous and detailed to list in a book of this type. However, there are five main areas on which you should concentrate during your inspection:

- the external appearance of the car including the bodywork, the tyres and the lights

- under the bonnet

- inside the car including the seats, windows and doors, the carpets (and underneath them) and the pedals

- how the car starts. Check the electrics at this point too, including lights, indicators, horn, windscreen washer and wiper and heater.

- how the car drives. Drive it for long enough to see how it behaves when the engine is warm as well as cold. Listen for any strange noises. Drive it at various speeds, on hills, round corners. Do an emergency stop and a hill start.

Independent inspections

You wouldn't dream of buying a house without asking a surveyor to look it over first and arguably you should take the same kind of precautions when you purchase a car. The AA and RAC will carry out a complete inspection and will give you an idea of whether the car is a good or a bad buy. The AA offers this service to their members only; the RAC to anybody. How long it takes to arrange an inspection depends on where you live – it may be as little as a day or longer than a week. This may prove a problem as private sellers in particular may be reluctant to wait. Obviously an independent test costs money so give the car the once-over yourself to make sure it is worth calling in the experts.

Before you clinch the deal

Buying a secondhand car is not so much a straightforward purchase as a deal: you are buying a package of good and bad points and you negotiate what you are prepared to pay for this. Make sure before you agree to buy that you know exactly what the deal is. If the garage tells you, or you discover, that the gearbox will need replacing before long, and that there's a dent on the rear bumper, get it in writing whether these points are going to be fixed before you take possession. Otherwise you may find that the over-eager salesman has made promises which his boss disapproves of and refuses to honour.

Finally . . .
When you have bought the car, keep every document connected with it together in a safe place in case anything goes wrong. Your file should include any advertisement for the car, the invoice and receipt, the cheque counterfoil or credit agreement, the warranty, service information and documents, registration documents and the MOT certificate.

Warranties and Guarantees

New cars
Warranties on new cars are offered by manufacturers as a marketing ploy to convince you of their products' reliability. They are none the less a useful addition to your legal rights when things go wrong, as they all-too-often do: when the OFT surveyed new car buyers it found that one in five had discovered what they considered to be significant faults with their vehicle.

However, the warranty does not give the blanket protection some people think. It is meant to cover defects in the manufacture and materials and not ordinary wear and tear – arguments can arise when *you* claim the problem is caused by a fault and *they* blame your driving. Bear in mind too that during the warranty period you will be expected to have the car serviced and repaired by a dealer franchised for that make.

Used cars
Guarantees on secondhand cars range from three months to a year or more. Some are offered by the dealer and others backed by manufacturers. The cover they provide varies considerably too. Some short-term dealers' guarantees exclude the very parts most likely to give trouble; others do not cover labour costs. Manufacturers' guarantees tend to be more comprehensive. A dealer's guarantee is only as good as the garage which gives it and some unscrupulous ones will try to fob you off with useless repairs until the guarantee has run out. Ask for confirmation of the guarantee in writing. Remember that you do not have to rely on a guarantee if things go wrong: you still have your legal rights (see below, pages 174–7).

Extended warranties
Extended warranties are intended to cover you when the original guarantee runs out. If you take out an extended warranty, check:

* exactly what it covers. Wear and tear will be excluded and some parts may not be covered. Is towage included, and hire of another vehicle while yours is off the road? Will you be reimbursed for the full cost of parts and labour? Under some schemes you are refunded only a proportion of the replacement costs depending on how long the part that failed would normally have been expected to last. Other schemes have a limit on how often and how much you can claim. You may have to pay a proportion of any claim you make.

* what the procedure is for making a claim. Do you have to go to an approved dealer and obtain authorisation before work on repairing your car can be started?

* whether the warranty is underwritten by an insurance company. There have been a number of cases where consumers have taken out extended guarantees (usually arranged through dealers on secondhand cars) and have tried to make a claim only to find that the company

which provided the warranty has disappeared without trace or has not forwarded the documents to the insurance company. To protect yourself against this kind of fraud, ask which insurance company is backing the warranty. Then contact the Department of Trade's Insurance Division and check that the insurance company is authorised for Class 16 insurance. Once you have taken out the warranty it may be wise to check that the insurers have actually received your premium.

What to Do if Things Go Wrong

New cars
If cars are grown-ups' toys, then discovering there is something wrong with your new vehicle is like opening a train set and finding that the batteries are missing. Resist the temptation to stamp your feet and remember that you have just the same rights under the Sale of Goods Act 1979 when you buy a car as you do when you purchase any other goods – in other words it must be *as described, of merchantable quality* and *fit for its purpose* (see Chapter 3).

* As soon as you discover the fault, go back to the garage where you bought the car. They may well be prepared to sort the problem out under the warranty. If a major defect develops after the warranty has expired, do not despair. The manufacturer or dealer may still be willing to do a warranty repair and, if not, you may still be able to make a claim under the Sale of Goods Act.

If, soon after you've bought the car, a problem – or series of problems – develops that is so serious that you decide you want to reject the vehicle and claim a refund, let the dealer know immediately and do not drive the car.

The warranty does not normally automatically cover you for the cost of hiring another car while yours is off the road, but manufacturers and dealers usually agree the circumstances in which they will pay for alternative transport. Whether you are legally entitled to claim the cost of hire depends on the seriousness of the problem,

how soon it occurs after purchase and the length of time
the car is off the road.

* If you cannot sort the problem out with the dealer,
  write to the managing director of the company at the
  dealership's head office.

* If you get nowhere and the car is still under warranty,
  contact the manufacturer. It may be worth contacting
  the manufacturer even if the warranty has expired, as
  he may put pressure on the dealer to sort the problem
  out.

* If you still have no success, seek advice from a Consumer Advice Centre or Citizens' Advice Bureau. If you
  are a member of one of the motoring organisations,
  they will take up your case.

* If you get nowhere and the dealer is a member of a trade
  association, write to the association outlining your
  complaint, the steps you have taken to resolve it so far
  and what you would like done. Trade associations that
  subscribe to the Code of Practice backed by the OFT
  have conciliation schemes to help sort out complaints
  between their members and their customers and you
  stand a reasonable chance of getting some satisfaction.
  Complaints about new cars are dealt with by the
  Customer Relations Adviser at the Society of Motor
  Manufacturers and Traders. A National Conciliation
  Service has recently been set up by the Motor Agents'
  Association and it is hoped that in time all the major
  trade associations dealing with cars and motorcycles
  will subscribe to this one scheme.

* If your problem is a serious one, consider arranging an
  independent inspection of the car through one of the
  motoring organisations (see above, page 171). This
  could strengthen your case if you end up in court or
  arbitration.

* If you have paid by credit, the finance company is
  equally responsible if things go wrong. If you cannot

resolve the matter with the manufacturer and dealer, take it up with them (see Chapter 11, pages 221–3).

* If you are still unhappy, you will have to decide whether to take the matter to court or to arbitration (see Chapter 13).

Used cars

FROM A GARAGE

When you buy a secondhand car from a dealer you have the same basic rights under the Sale of Goods Act as if you had bought new. However, you obviously cannot expect a used car to be in perfect condition. Whether you are entitled to compensation when things go wrong will depend on:

- the age of the car
- what you paid for it
- how long you've had it
- what knd of use it has had in that time
- how serious the fault is.

Basically, the older the car and the less you paid, the less you can expect. Remember, you are not entitled to compensation for any faults which you were told about or, if you examined the car, which you should have noticed during that examination.

The steps for complaining about a used car are basically the same as those for new cars (see above), although the manufacturer will not normally be involved unless the car is under a manufacturer's warranty. It is especially important to sort out in advance exactly who is going to pay for any repairs that have to be carried out. If a serious fault develops soon after purchase, and you agree to try to have it fixed by the garage, make it clear – preferably in writing – that if the repair is unsatisfactory you reserve your right to reject the car completely and claim a refund.

If the trader made a false statement about the car which helped persuade you to buy it, you may have a case against him for misrepresentation. If you are sold a car which is unroadworthy, the trader must tell you that it is suitable only for breaking up; otherwise he has committed an offence under the Road Traffic Act 1972 and you should tell the police.

Alec Smart bought a two-year-old saloon car advertised as being 'in excellent condition' from a dealer who offered a three-month warranty. After two months the clutch failed and rust spots began to appear. Alec returned to the garage. The dealer pointed out that neither the clutch nor bodywork were covered under terms of the warranty and refused to repair the car without charge. Alec sued the garage under the Sale of Goods Act, on the grounds that the car was not *of merchantable quality*, and for misrepresentation as the dealer had made a false statement about the car's condition. The court awarded him the cost of a new clutch and compensation for the poor condition of the car.

FROM AN AUCTION

If something goes wrong with a car you've bought at auction there is little you can do unless it was sold 'with warranty' or 'with no major mechanical faults'. In this case you must register your complaint within the agreed period and you may be entitled to compensation or a refund. Your rights at auction are very limited and depend on the Conditions of Sale.

WHEN YOU HAVE BOUGHT PRIVATELY

Goods bought privately must be 'as described', but they do not have to be of 'merchantable quality' or 'fit for their purpose'. If the seller knowingly made a false statement about the car, you may be able to sue for misrepresentation but this can be difficult to prove if the seller is uncooperative and you have no witnesses and nothing in writing (see Chapter 3, page 55).

The Trade Descriptions Act does not apply to private sales. The Road Traffic Act does apply.

Servicing and Repairs

For those who know nothing about cars, having a service or repair carried out feels a bit like handing a blank cheque to the garage owner. Not only is it hard to know whether the work has been done properly, it may be impossible to tell whether it has been done at all. Research by the OFT suggests that one customer in ten has a complaint about garage servicing. Put one way, that means that about 90 per cent of customers are satisfied. Put another, it means that 1½ million people a year are not.

Predictably, the main causes of complaint seem to be that garages don't do all the necessary work or do not do it properly or charge too much. When trading standards officers in the West Midlands took a car with known faults to a number of franchised dealers for a full service according to the manufacturer's schedule, they found that none completed the service to the manufacturer's specifications and one missed potentially dangerous problems.

So what can you do to make sure that you get the service you pay for? First, choose your garage with care and, secondly, use it properly. There's no doubt that many complaints arise because of misunderstandings or a lack of communication between customer and trader.

How to choose a garage

Start by asking your friends in the area whether they would recommend the garage they use. When choosing, look for one that:

- looks clean and where the staff – from the receptionists upwards – are friendly and obliging
- gives estimates or displays menu-price lists for the most common jobs
- guarantees its workmanship and materials
- can fit a job in quickly when necessary
- is easy to get to and from
- checks its mechanics' work. In most garages mechanics are paid a bonus if they finish a job in much less time

than the manufacturer allows in his service schedule. This system has come under fire because it rewards speed rather than quality of work. Ask if the garage runs such an incentive scheme for its mechanics and, if so, what quality control checks it operates.

Although motorists use franchised dealers for repairs under warranty, there is evidence to suggest that once this has expired they switch to smaller specialist service and repair garages with a more personal approach and – sometimes – lower charges. On average, customers seem to be more satisfied with these than with the larger, franchised garages.

Garages appointed by the motoring organisations – the AA and the RAC – are inspected and approved by them, so in theory at least you should be able to expect a reasonable standard of service.

If you choose a garage which belongs to a trade association with a code of practice backed by the OFT, you have some extra protection and the safety-net of a conciliation service if you are dissatisfied. (The Motor Agents' Association has actually produced a booklet for its members called 'How to Achieve Customer Satisfaction in Vehicle Servicing and Repair'.) However, research by the OFT suggests you are no more likely to be satisfied with a trade association member garage than any other.

How to use your garage
If you seem to be indifferent to what is happening to your car, then do not be surprised if the garage reflects your own lack of interest. You don't have to be a fusspot, but **show you care.** If you want to get the best out of your chosen garage, follow the 'buy-laws':

☞ Tell the garage exactly what you want them to do, preferably in writing. **Don't** just dash in, fling your keys on the desk and dash out again to catch the train to work or your lift back home. If you want a service according to the manufacturer's schedule, say so. And make sure you know what this involves – some services are more comprehensive than others. If you ask for a service, you cannot expect the garage to discover that your cigar lighter does not work or that the car is a poor starter on damp mornings. So, if there are any specific problems that need attention, write them down and hand the list to the receptionist (don't just leave it in the car). The important thing is to make sure that the mechanic gets the message. Be prepared to spend time demonstrating any faults which are not obvious.

☞ Ask for an estimate or quotation, preferably in writing, and make sure it includes parts, labour and VAT. Check whether or not you are being given a firm price for the job. Many garages now display 'menus' with prices for a wide range of jobs, which should reduce disputes over charges. If the price seems high, ring around a few other garages and compare.

☞ Make it clear what you want the garage to do if the job turns out to be more expensive than estimated and leave a telephone number where you can be contacted. Otherwise you cannot blame them if they do not do essential work which you did not authorise; you do not have to pay for anything done without your approval.

> Simon Simple left his six-year-old car at his local garage for an MOT. He told the manager he wanted it to pass because he was taking it on holiday the following day and authorised him to do everything necessary to bring it up to scratch. He was fairly confident that the car was in good condition and did not bother to leave a telephone number where he could be reached. When he returned, the garage presented him with a bill for £300 – half the value of the car. Simon was furious and considered suing, but when he asked other garages what they would have charged for the same work, he found the price he had paid was quite reasonable. As he had authorised the work, there was nothing he could do.

☞ Find out how long the job will take. It is wise to ring the garage to check that the car is ready before you set off to collect it.

☞ Ask for a detailed invoice listing all the work carried out and the cost of parts and labour. Go over this carefully and do not be afraid to query anything which is not clear. If you have paid for new parts, have a look under the bonnet to make sure the old ones *have* been replaced and ask the garage to give you the old parts – the Code of Practice says trade association members should do this.

What to do if things go wrong
Under the Supply of Goods and Services Act, any work carried out by a garage must be of a reasonable standard and – unless otherwise agreed – must be done within a reasonable time and at a reasonable charge.

* If you have a complaint when you come to collect the car, try to sort it out on the spot. If you cannot, you have a problem – the garage has your car and you want it back. So you will normally have to pay first and argue later. If you are unhappy about some aspect of the work, write on the invoice 'paid under protest' and make sure both you and the garage keep a copy.

* The steps for pursuing a complaint are basically the same as those for dealing with a problem with a new car (see above, pages 174–6), but the manufacturer will not be involved unless the work is done under warranty.

The Code of Practice for the Motor Industry

NEW CARS

● Any price quoted in an advertisement should be the 'on-the-road' price. If extras are not included, the advertisement should make this clear.

- A pre-delivery inspection should be carried out and the dealer should give you a copy of the checklist.

- You should be told what the manufacturer's warranty covers and given a copy. The warranty should be easy to understand and you should be given advice on what to do if you have a problem with a part not covered by the warranty. Dealers should be given guidelines by the manufacturer on when they can let a customer have a loan car while his vehicle is off the road. If you sell the car during the warranty period, the warranty should be transferable to the new owner.

USED CARS

- Cars should be given a pre-sales inspection by the garage and a checklist revealing any faults should be displayed inside the car. The buyer should also be given a copy.

- You should be given reasonable facilities to examine the car yourself or to get somebody else to do it for you.

- The dealer should set out in writing any promises he makes about the car or any guarantees he gives.

- You should be told if the car's mileage reading cannot be verified.

SERVICING AND REPAIRS

- You should be given an estimate of the cost of parts and labour for all major repairs and manufacturers' recommended servicing. If possible you should be given a firm quotation in writing. You should be told whether the quoted price is a firm one or not.

- Unless the repair is carried out under warranty or replacement parts are being supplied on an exchange basis, you will be able to take away any old parts which have been replaced.

- You should be given a clear invoice with details of the work done and the materials used.

- Garages should not display disclaimers which try to avoid liability for loss or damage to your car.

- Repairs must be guaranteed against poor workmanship and the length of the guarantee should be on the invoice.

- Garages must take responsibility for any work which they sub-contract.

Three trade associations subscribe to this Code of Practice. They are the Motor Agents' Association, the Society of Motor Manufacturers and Traders, and the Scottish Motor Trade Association. The Vehicle Builders' and Repairers' Association deals only with body repairs for cars and caravans and also has a code of practice backed by the OFT.

Motorcycles
Four trade associations involved in the sale and repair of motor cycles have drawn up a code of practice backed by the OFT with similar provisions to those listed above. These are the Motor Cycle Association, the Motor Agents' Association, the Scottish Motor Trade Association and the Motorcycle Retailers' Association.

10

You and Your Home

The life-cycle experts rate moving home, along with getting married, having a baby and changing your job, as one of the more stressful of life's experiences and anybody who has been through this particular adventure will have no difficulty in seeing why.

Even if you are one of those rare and blessed mortals for whom everything goes smoothly from start to finish, the process can be exhausting. If you are less fortunate, moving home can leave you vowing to be a snail or a hermit crab in your next incarnation.

It is impossible to go into the subject in depth here – whole books have been written on this topic alone. My aim is to simplify some of the main steps, point to the pitfalls and generally help you to make the right decisions when you move.

Selling Your Home

Estate agents: how to choose
Estate agents as a group have acquired a reputation for doing relatively little and charging a great deal for it. They argue in reply that, although some homes do sell quickly and with little effort on their part, others require a good deal of work and – if they are ultimately sold through another agent – may bring in no money at all.

You may resent their charges but the fact is that, at present, people looking for a new home tend to go to estate agents, so giving the profession a tidy slice, though not a monopoly, of the home-selling market. If you do decide to use an agent – and I look at the alternatives below – you will want to go to one who will leave you feeling that his fee was cash well spent, rather than money for old rope. Before you choose, follow the 'buy-laws':

☞ Get three or four valuations of your home from different agents. Make sure you do not have to pay for these. Do not automatically go for the agent who has given you the highest valuation: he may have over-valued in order to gain your custom and may later suggest that you drop the price.

☞ Compare the commission charged by different firms. It is against the law for estate agents in a particular area to agree to charge the same fee. Nevertheless, in some areas you will find little variation in charges while in others there are quite big differences. If you think one agent's commission is excessive, try to negotiate with him. Remember to ask if you have to pay for any 'extras' such as newspaper advertising, photographs, or having a board erected.

☞ You can tell a good deal about a firm just from a visit to their office. You want one which is going to work hard at selling your home. Do they seem interested, lively, on-the-ball? Or do the staff look half-dead behind their desks, barely mustering enough enthusiasm to glance up as you approach? Do you see their boards in the area, their ads in the local paper? Do they come round promptly to give you a valuation? And do they sell your type of property? You wouldn't take your ten-year-old Mini to a Rolls-Royce dealer: don't offer your suburban flat to an agent who specialises in country mansions.

☞ Members of one of the professional bodies – the Royal Institution of Chartered Surveyors (RICS), the Incorporated Society of Valuers and Auctioneers (ISVA) and the National Association of Estate Agents (NAEA) – must adhere to a code of professional conduct and meet certain entry requirements (members of the RICS and the ISVA have to undergo training and pass a series of exams; admission to the NAEA depends on experience and interview). All three organisations operate bonding schemes which protect buyers' money if one of their members goes bankrupt or runs off with customers' deposits. They all have procedures for dealing with consumers' complaints. Agents who don't belong to one of these organisations are not bound by a code of professional ethics; you would lose your money if you handed over a deposit to such an agent and he disappeared.

The Estate Agents Act 1979
The Act says that estate agents must:

- tell you in advance what their fees will be and when you will have to pay them; they don't have to do this in writing
- tell buyers if they or their associates have a personal interest in a particular property
- hold buyers' deposits in a special client account and pay interest if they are holding more than £500 and the interest amounts to more than £10.

The Director General of Fair Trading can ban an agent from practice if he is found to be 'unfit' – because he has committed fraud perhaps, or broken the Estate Agents Act.

Understanding estate agents' jargon

Sole agency means you instruct only one agent. In some parts of the country you have to use this system; in others you can choose how many agents you instruct. The advantages of sole agency are that you pay less commission because the agent knows he is not going to lose the sale to another firm. For the same reason he is likely to put in more effort. Only give a firm sole agency for a limited period – say two–four weeks. If they haven't found a buyer within that time, you are free to go to other agents.

Joint sole agency means you instruct more than one agent – with the agreement of each of the firms involved – and they decide between them how the commission is to be split. You will normally pay more than if one firm had sole agency but less than for multiple agency.

Multiple agency means you instruct as many agents as you like independently of each other. The one who sells your home gets the commission.

Never give an agent **sole selling rights.** You will have to pay him commission even if you manage to sell your home without his help.

Don't agree to pay an agent commission unless he introduces the person who buys your home. If the firm expects a fee simply for finding a buyer who is **ready, willing and able** to purchase, stay away: you could be asked to pay commission even if the deal falls through.

Simon Simple decided to move and instructed a local agent. The firm said they would charge only ¾ per cent commission if he gave them sole selling rights. As other agents in the area were asking 1½ per cent commission, and Simon did not want to spend more money than he had to, he agreed. A few days later, his neighbour told him he knew somebody who was looking for a house in the area. The man offered Simon a good price and the deal went through. Simon was just congratulating himself on having saved himself the agent's fees when he received a bill for their commission. Because he had given them sole selling rights, he had to pay, even though they were not involved in the sale in any way.

Complaining about an estate agent

* If you have a complaint about an estate agent, write to one of the senior partners of the firm (you'll find their name near the top of the list on their headed notepaper) – at the head office if it is part of a chain – explaining what has gone wrong and indicating what solution you want. Include all relevant details in your letter, such as the addresses of the properties involved, the names of the owners and the events (with dates) that led to the problem.

* If you are unhappy with the response, seek advice from a Consumer Advice Centre or Citizens' Advice Bureau.

* If you think the firm has breached the Estate Agents Act, tell the trading standards or consumer protection department at your local council offices.

* If one of the partners in the firm belongs to a professional organisation (you can tell whether he does from the letters after his name on the firm's stationery), write to that organisation outlining your complaint and asking them to investigate.

* If you still have no success or if you think the estate agent has been negligent and you are seeking compensation, you will have to consider legal action (see Chapter 13).

If you don't want to use an estate agent

There *are* other ways of selling your home. The advantage of them all is that – if they work – they will cost you far less than an estate agent's commission. The disadvantages are that:

● you will have to get your home valued yourself

● in general you have to pay regardless of whether you sell your property this way

- you will not usually get any help if, once a buyer has been found, the negotiations on price prove to be tricky. If you find haggling over money embarrassing, you may be happier using an agent – though it must be said that not all agents put in much effort at this stage either.

Property shops display details of your home at their offices and may send particulars to potential buyers – much as an estate agent does. They usually make a one-off charge for putting your home on their books or bill you monthly. What you get for your money varies a good deal: in some cases you have to prepare the particulars yourself, in others the shop will help you. Sometimes the costs of a 'For Sale' board and local newspaper advertising are included in the price, sometimes they are not.

Computerised introduction services work a bit like dating agencies, matching homes with buyers. You pay a flat fee (the size may depend on the value of your property) and fill out a form giving details of your home. If your place is unusual or difficult to sell without a salesman's persuasive touch, this method is probably not for you. Ask how long the property remains on the computer.

Newspaper advertisements leave everything to you. National newspaper advertising is expensive – and probably only worthwhile if the property columns often carry ads for homes in your area. If you advertise in a local paper, make your entry eye-catching: remember, you are competing for attention with the estate agents. One photograph may be worth many words. It is also a good idea to prepare photocopied particulars of the place for prospective buyers to take away.

Recent changes
The way in which we buy and sell our homes is likely to change over the next few years thanks to new legislation and the relaxation of some of the rules controlling

the way professionals operate. For example, solicitors in England and Wales have joined their Scottish colleagues and become involved in estate agency. Banks have also entered the estate agency business, and the passing of the Building Societies Act 1986 will see these organisations offering a more varied package of house-buying services than before. Instead of having to visit estate agents, solicitors, surveyors, and sources of finance and insurance separately, we will be able to do 'one-stop' shopping when we buy and sell our homes. These changes *should* increase competition and make the business of moving simpler and cheaper for consumers. However, if a wide variety of services is offered under one roof, it will be more important than ever to shop around for the best deal before you choose where to take your business. Do not make the mistake of swallowing a package whole, just because it is convenient. Do not, for example, put your house with the estate agency run by your building society just because you are getting a mortgage from them, if they have a poor reputation for selling homes.

Buying a Home: Step-by-Step

☞ Work out how much you want to borrow and can afford to repay each month. Have your present property valued and approach possible sources of finance (see below, page 201) to find out the total you can spend on your new home. Remember to include estate agents', solicitors', surveyors', removers' and Land Registry fees, stamp duty and fittings for your new home in your calculations. Arrange your finance 'in principle'.

☞ Leave your name with all estate agents in your chosen area(s) and scan the local newspapers. Don't be afraid to look at properties above your price range, especially when there are more homes around than buyers. If you make a low offer at a time like this the worst you will be faced with is derisive laughter. On the other hand, if the market is busy you may have to offer the asking price as soon as you see a property you like. If there's not much on the market, badger the estate agents – you want them to remember *your* face when the property of your dreams comes onto their books. Always take estate agents' particulars with a few handfuls of salt. They are not covered by the Trade Descriptions Act and can often be misleading.

☞ Once you've made an offer which has been accepted, apply formally for a mortgage, arrange to have a survey carried out and find a solicitor or conveyancer to handle the legal side (see below for more detail on these steps).

☞ Don't assume that once your offer has been accepted, all will be plain sailing. The sellers may well keep the house on the market in case the deal with you falls through, or they may be hoping for a better offer. It's vital at this stage to maintain a good and regular relationship with the estate agent and the seller. Without becoming a nuisance – and only if the seller is willing – visit your prospective home a couple of times, ostensibly to measure up for curtains and carpets, but really so that the owners get to know you and would feel bad about stabbing you in the back and selling to somebody else. Don't fall out over small things like the cost of buying their washing machine or light fittings. If you can't agree, drop the matter.

☞ Provided the survey and solicitor's enquiries reveal no hiccups, your solicitor will send you the contracts on your sale and purchase for you to sign. At this stage you pay a 10 per cent deposit to the seller's solicitor. You are now responsible for insuring your new home.

☞ Get estimates from two or three removal firms. Costs vary considerably but, before you plump for the cheapest, check what is included in the price otherwise you could end up paying extra for tea chests or for packing. Make sure your belongings will be fully insured during the move. The British Association of Removers (BAR) keeps an eye on its members' work and investigates complaints about member companies from consumers.

☞ About a month after exchange of contracts you will complete the purchase and move home.

Scotland

The procedure for buying a house in Scotland is rather different. Once you make an offer which is accepted, it is binding on both parties, so you should have a survey done and apply for a mortgage *before* making your offer.

Briefly, the system works like this:

- The seller fixes a date by which all offers on his home must be received. He also decides upon a minimum price he will consider.

- Once you have found a home you like, instruct your solicitor to 'note interest' with the seller's solicitor.

- If the survey is favourable and the building society will lend you what you want, discuss with your solicitor how much more than the minimum you should offer and instruct him to make an offer on your behalf. If this is accepted, the house will be yours.

- Over the ensuing weeks your solicitor will examine the title deeds and prepare a draft conveyance, transferring the property to your name. Meanwhile you should make arrangements to move.

- On the 'date of entry', you pay the purchase price in full and collect the keys.

Buying a flat

If you're intending to buy a flat there are particular pitfalls you should look out for. One of the biggest headaches for flat-dwellers is who takes responsibility for carrying out maintenance and repairs and how these are funded and organised. Your dream flat can become a nightmare if a week after you move in you discover that the roof and lifts need replacing and that the landlord who is supposed to organise this work refuses to do so and instead has the lobby repapered in silk and sends the bill to the residents. To guard against such horror stories find out:

* who is responsible for maintenance and repairs and whether these are promptly and efficiently carried out. If you think the seller is not being entirely honest with you, ask existing residents. Find out what say the residents have in the way maintenance and repairs are carried out.

* what the service charge is, what it covers and when it is paid.

* whether a firm of managing agents supervises services and maintenance in the block and whether they are efficient.

* whether there are likely to be any major items of expenditure in the near future such as new lifts, central heating, or redecoration (your surveyor will advise on this) and, if so, how these will be funded. Find out whether there is a sinking fund for major items of expenditure, how much goes into it, what it covers and how the money is invested. If there is no such fund, you could be faced with a huge bill every time the outside needs repainting.

* who insures the building and whether the cover is adequate.

Buying a newly built house
The advantages of buying a new house are fairly obvious. You will have modern fixtures and fittings, possibly of your choice, better insulation, and hopefully fewer maintenance expenses than with a second-hand house. However, it pays to choose your builder with care: surveys carried out for the National House Building Council (NHBC) show that on a good estate 70–80 per cent of homeowners are prepared to recom-

mend their builder whereas on poor estates the figure
may be as low as 30 per cent. The NHBC has also found
that there are fewer complaints about firms that have a
national reputation or are well-known locally. Before
you buy:

* Find out what you can about the builder's reputation –
  if possible by talking to people who have bought his
  houses.

* Take a good look at the site. Is it tidy, with building
  materials kept clean and dry?

* Ask other residents on the estate what they do and do
  not like about their homes.

* Find out from the other residents how prompt the
  builder is at attending to faults. Does he do a routine
  maintenance check?

* Don't let yourself be swayed too much by the builder's
  'special offers', such as reductions on the mortgage or
  schemes which pay your mortgage if you lose your job.
  Remember, all these perks have to be paid for by you in
  the house purchase price. And they are only worth
  having if you're getting a well-built home too.

THE NHBC PROTECTION SCHEME
Houses built by one of the 20,000 or so builders registered with the NHBC must conform to the Council's
requirements and are inspected during construction.
They are then covered by the Ten Year Protection
Scheme. During the first two years the builder will
correct any faults caused by his failure to meet NHBC
standards. Normal shrinkage and wear and tear are
excluded and electrical installations and central heating
boilers are only covered for one year. If the builder is
uncooperative, you can contact the NHBC's conciliation and arbitration service. From the third to the tenth
year after the house is built, the NHBC scheme insures
you against major damage caused by structural defects.

If the builder has gone out of business, you are still protected under the Ten Year Scheme.

The Survey

If you are applying for a mortgage, the financial institution which is lending you the money – normally a bank or building society – will send a surveyor to value your prospective home. On the basis of his report, the building society decides how much it can lend you. If there are serious structural problems, it may refuse you a mortgage completely on that property, or may withhold a proportion of the loan.

Although you have to pay for this valuation, and some building societies will let you see a copy, it is of no real use to you as a prospective purchaser. The fact that the building society will grant you a mortgage does not mean the house is necessarily structurally sound, problem free or worth what you are paying for it. And if there *are* any defects which the building society's surveyor fails to spot you are very unlikely to have a case against him because he has no responsibility to you.

You should therefore have a survey carried out for your own benefit. There are various ways of going about this.

* When you apply for a mortgage, you can ask the building society to arrange for their surveyor to carry out a survey for you. This should save you money because only one surveyor has to visit your home. The disadvantage is that you may not be able to choose who does the survey and may not be able to discuss the findings with him afterwards. Also, you will not have any say over *when* the survey is carried out, so if you are in a hurry, because there are other buyers after the house, you may be wise to 'go independent'. If you do use a building society surveyor, check that he is responsible to you (and not just to the society) if he makes a mistake.

* If you decide to use your own surveyor, choose one who works in the area of your prospective home. He'll

know more about house values in that area and also about local factors, such as subsidence, which may affect the property. Ask friends if they can recommend a surveyor. Your solicitor and estate agent may also be able to help. Use only a surveyor trained by one of the professional bodies. The Information Centre at the Royal Institution of Chartered Surveyors (RICS), the Secretary at the Incorporated Society of Valuers and Auctioneers (ISVA), and the Incorporated Association of Architects and Surveyors (IAAS) can give you names of qualified surveyors in your area.

There are two types of survey:

- A **full structural survey** covers everything that is 'reasonably visible', including roof spaces where there is a trapdoor, outside roofs where practicable, drains, floorboards, electrics, and central heating. But the surveyor won't risk damaging somebody else's home, so he will not be able to look under a ceramic tiled kitchen floor to examine the boards, or open windows which are stuck together with paint. If there is anything you particularly want the surveyor to investigate, tell him in advance. Tell him, too, if there are any changes you would like to make to the house, so he can advise on whether they are practical.

- In the last few years a new type of survey has been introduced, less thorough and less expensive than a full structural survey but probably adequate for most properties. You cannot have this kind of survey done on a very large or very old house. A **house or flat buyer's report and valuation** covers parts of the property that are 'readily visible or accessible'. It will highlight major problems but it won't give you detailed advice on what repairs are likely to be needed over the next few years. Before you decide which kind of survey to have, compare prices. If there is little difference you might as well opt for the most thorough inspection.

What to do if things go wrong

* If a surveyor gives your new home a clean bill of health and you move in only to find that the place is rapidly sinking into a bog or that you could grow mustard and cress on the bathroom walls, call the surveyor back. If he dismisses your fears, or denies responsibility, you will have to consider suing for negligence or breach of contract (see Chapter 13). All surveyors are insured against negligence so you will get your money if you win.

> Alec Smart employed a surveyor to carry out a full structural survey on the house he wanted to buy. The surveyor found no major problems and Alec went ahead with the purchase. Six months after moving in, Alec lifted up the carpet in the spare bedroom and discovered something that looked suspiciously like dry rot. He called in a specialist treatment firm who confirmed that the floorboards were indeed rotten and would cost at least £1,200 to treat. The surveyor denied liability, so Alec took him to court. The court found that the surveyor had been negligent and awarded Alec £1,200 damages.

If your complaint concerns some other aspect of the service provided by a surveyor, such as delay in dealing with your work, disclosing confidential information about your affairs without your permission or not replying to your letters, try to sort out the problem with the firm itself. If you have no success, write to the surveyor's professional body, describing clearly, with dates, what work the surveyor did for you and explaining why you are dissatisfied. They will investigate your complaint and, if necessary, discipline the member concerned. They will not deal with complaints of professional negligence or award compensation.

The Conveyancing

The legal side of buying or selling a property is called conveyancing and has traditionally been carried out by solicitors. However, you do have other options: you can do the work yourself, or employ a non-solicitor conveyancer.

Solicitors versus conveyancers

Predictably enough, solicitors view themselves as the only people who are fully competent to carry out conveyancing, and until recently it was certainly true that it was only by using a solicitor that you could be absolutely sure that you, your money and your property were protected against negligence, fraud or dishonesty. However, thanks to recent changes in the law, from Spring 1987 you will have comparable protection when you use a licensed conveyancer.

The position now is that conveyancing may only be carried out for gain by:

- solicitors
- conveyancers who are approved by the Council of Licensed Conveyancers
- barristers
- duly certificated notaries public.

In practice, the last two categories rarely do conveyancing.

Other people may offer 'conveyancing services' (though legally they would have to arrange for certain parts of the transaction to be done by a licensed conveyancer or solicitor), but if you use them you may have no protection if things go wrong, so you should steer clear.

SOLICITORS

The advantage of using a solicitor is that he has an all-round legal training and background and should be able to spot and sort out any problems as they occur. The vast majority of conveyances are utterly routine, but if yours is not you may be glad of your solicitor's

expertise. A solicitor can also advise on other matters –
such as drawing up a will – which may concern you at
this time, and can sometimes help with arranging a
mortgage or finding a surveyor.

The main reason for not using a solicitor is usually
the size of his bill. In the past this was often several
times that of conveyancing firms, but increased competition has brought fees down quite dramatically.
Whereas solicitors used to charge a percentage of the
sale and purchase price of the property, they now
tend to be more flexible. Some still use the percentage
system, others base their charges on the amount of
work involved, and an increasing number levy a flat fee
regardless of how complicated the transaction is. To get
estimates of the likely cost, ring a few firms and look in
the local newspaper, where some solicitors advertise
their charges. Bear in mind that if you pay a rock
bottom price you will get a 'no frills' service. If you are
the sort who likes his solicitor to keep him in touch
every step of the way, you must expect to pay a little
more.

LICENSED CONVEYANCERS

Licensed conveyancers boast that they are the special-
ists when it comes to the sale and purchase of property
and that when you use them you *know* you are dealing
with somebody experienced in this field, whereas a
solicitor may hand the work over to an unqualified
clerk. You no more need a solicitor for conveyancing,
they insist, than you need a brain surgeon when you
have a headache. (The solicitors reply that, for an unfortunate few, the headache turns out to be a brain tumour
and to require rather more complicated treatment than
was first thought.)

In the past some solicitors have been reluctant to
cooperate with conveyancers representing the other
side in a transaction, and building societies have
refused to let non-solicitors act for them in a house
purchase (normally your solicitor will act for both you
and whoever is lending you the finance). However, the
advent of licensing should mean that the suspicion of
non-solicitor conveyancers gradually evaporates.

Choosing a conveyancer used to be something of a lottery, but licensing should change that. Anybody granted a licence must comply with the standards of training and rules on consumer protection laid down by the Council of Licensed Conveyancers. The Council keeps a register of licensed conveyancers which you can ask to see. It will also investigate complaints against licensed conveyancers and discipline them when necessary. It has the power to withdraw a conveyancer's licence when appropriate.

Doing it yourself

Understandably, the professionals liken doing your own conveyancing to treating your headache with nothing more than a cold compress. But many people have done the job successfully themselves and saved several hundred pounds in the process. There are now a number of books on the market to guide you through the maze. The main drawbacks to doing it yourself are that it takes time, involves a great deal of form-filling and paperwork and if things get complicated you may have to hand over to a professional half way through. If you are getting a mortgage, you will have to pay the bank or building society's legal fees in any case, as they will not let you act for them.

If time is short, or you are worried that you may make some appalling mistake which will mean you don't actually own your house at the end of the day, you could deal with the sale and let a professional handle the purchase – though check first what the savings are likely to be. In any event, you would be unwise to tackle the conveyancing if:

- you are buying a flat or a leasehold house
- the property is not registered
- there is a sitting tenant
- the house is newly built
- the owners are divorcing.

All these situations can involve legal complications which are beyond the capabilities of most laymen. And when you are doing conveyancing the penalties for making a mistake can be severe.

The Mortgage

Perhaps the least pleasant aspect of home-buying is working out how much it is all going to cost you. At present *getting* a mortgage is not a problem: there are more lenders around than ever before. The difficult part is deciding where to obtain your mortgage and which type to choose.

Be warned!

You may well be offered a loan which is larger than you can comfortably afford to repay. Do not be tempted.

Who lends money?

You may be able to obtain a mortgage from:

- your employer
- a bank
- a building society
- an insurance company
- a finance company
- your local authority (if you are a council tenant wanting to buy your own home).

Your solicitor, accountant, bank manager or estate agent or a mortgage broker may be able to help you to obtain a mortgage, but make sure they are offering you the best deal for your needs.

Which type of mortgage?

REPAYMENT MORTGAGES

From the start you pay back some of the capital you have borrowed, together with interest on the unpaid part of the loan. At the beginning most of what you pay is interest; but the balance shifts as time goes on. Some lenders insist that you take out a mortgage protection policy so that the loan will be paid off if you die, but life insurance is not part of a repayment mortgage.

ENDOWMENT MORTGAGES

During the period of the loan you pay only interest to the building society but at the same time you pay a monthly premium to an insurance company. At the end of the loan period, the proceeds of the endowment policy pay off the capital you owe and there may be a bonus for you. If you die, the loan is automatically paid off.

There are three basic types of endowment mortgage:

- *non-profit* – the proceeds from the endowment policy are just enough to repay the loan with nothing left over.
- *with-profits* – the proceeds from the endowment policy pay off the loan and leave you with a lump sum. You obviously pay more for this bonus.
- *low-cost endowment* – it is assumed that the proceeds of the policy will more than cover the sum assured, so this sum is lower than the size of the loan. This means the premiums you pay are smaller. You cannot be absolutely certain that the policy will yield enough to pay off the loan and, if it did not, you would have to find the difference.

The main disadvantage of an endowment mortgage is that when interest rates increase you cannot usually extend the length of the loan in order to keep the repayments down. And this kind of mortgage may cost more. Before you choose one, you should also consider the implications if, as is very likely, you move before the loan is repaid.

PENSION-LINKED MORTGAGES

During the period of the loan, you pay only interest to the building society and at the same time you contribute to a personal pension plan. At the end of the loan period, the proceeds of the pension funds repay the capital you owe and give you a pension. You get tax relief on the pension contributions, as well as on the interest payments. Only the self-employed or those who do not belong to an employer's pension scheme are eligible for this kind of mortgage.

Before you choose
Before you decide what kind of mortgage to go for and where to get it, shop around and find out:

* whether the lender will give a mortgage on the kind of property in which you are interested. Some are less enthusiastic about properties with short leases or sitting tenants for example.

* whether mortgages are given only to savers or account holders with that particular bank or building society. When mortgages are tight, you may find banks less strict about this than building societies.

* what happens if you want to move before the loan is repaid. Are there any penalties for 'early redemption'?

* what happens if you cannot afford the repayments and what steps you can take to protect your family if you die before the loan is repaid.

  Then compare:

* not only the interest rates charged by different lenders, but also the monthly repayments and APRs (Annual Percentage Rate of the total charge for credit). The APR takes into account everything you have to pay for credit and how and when you pay and is the simplest way to compare different deals.

* the tax benefits of different types of mortgage.

* how much you can get. Lenders have different formulae for calculating the maximum they'll let you borrow, based on your income.

* what proportion of the value of the property you can borrow. Building societies may lend a higher proportion than banks and some societies will lend more than others.

Homeloan

First-time home-buyers can receive extra financial help under the government's Homeloan scheme. To qualify, you must have saved for at least two years with one of the institutions taking part in the scheme – these include many banks and building societies – and must have a certain amount in your account. Your account must be registered under the scheme. The help is available only to people who have never owned their own home before and who are buying lower-price properties. You can get more information from the Department of the Environment or from participating savings institutions.

Renting Your Home: Your Rights

The law concerning landlords and their tenants is a subject so complicated it makes even solicitors go pale. This section is intended to do no more than summarise your rights in the main problem areas. The Department of the Environment publishes a series of *Housing Booklets* which summarise the rights of different types of tenant. A similar series, covering Scotland, is available from the Scottish Development Department.

If you are asked to leave

* If you are in private rented accommodation, furnished or unfurnished, and the landlord does not live on the premises, you probably have a **regulated tenancy.** This means you have certain rights affecting your security of tenure.

    If you are a regulated tenant and your landlord wants you to leave, he must obtain a possession order from a court. This applies even if your tenancy agreement has come to an end. If your landlord tries to make you leave without a court order, tell your local authority. They may prosecute. In Scotland, you should tell the police, who may report the harassment to the Procurator Fiscal, with a view to prosecution.

If you have a **periodic tenancy** – i.e. your tenancy agreement runs week by week or month by month and not for a fixed term – the landlord must first serve you with a written notice to quit giving you at least four weeks in which to leave. He cannot apply for a possession order until the notice to quit has expired.

He does not have to serve a notice to quit if you have a **fixed-term tenancy** for a specific period which has come to an end.

In order to get a possession order from a court, the landlord must show that he has grounds for possession as set out in the Rent Acts. Normally, the landlord can only get a possession order if the tenant is in rent arrears, has broken the tenancy agreement or has damaged the property.

Simon Simple rented a furnished flat. One night he held a party during which a table lamp was smashed, red wine was poured all over the living room carpet and the settee was covered in cigarette burns. The landlord served a notice to quit on Simon who ignored it. The landlord then went to court to obtain a possession order. The landlord argued that it would be reasonable for the court to grant an order, and Simon argued that it would not. After considering the case, the court granted the order and gave Simon a month to leave because he had breached the clause in his tenancy agreement which said he had to keep the place in good repair.

---

* If your landlord lives on the premises you will not normally have full security of tenure. However, the landlord must still obtain a possession order from a court before he can evict you and if you have a *periodic*

tenancy he must first serve you with four weeks' notice
to quit in writing.

* If your home is owned by the council or by a housing
  association you usually have considerable security of
  tenure. If the council or housing association wants you
  to leave, it has to go through a similar series of steps to
  those described above for *regulated tenants*. The court
  may ask for an assurance that suitable alternative
  accommodation is available for you.

If the rent is too high

If you really think that you are paying too much rent, you
or your landlord or both of you can apply to have the rent
assessed and a **fair rent** registered. If you are a regulated
tenant you can do this by contacting the Rent Officer
(listed in the telephone directory under that name) and
filling out a form. You must say what you think a fair rent
would be, but the Rent Officer will decide for himself,
usually after inspecting the property and sometimes
after meeting you and the landlord. The Rent Officer
may fix a rent which is lower or higher than the one you
are paying now. You can get an idea of what he is likely to
decide by looking up recent rent registrations for similar
properties in the local Rent Register. If you or the
landlord disagree with the Rent Officer's decision, you
can appeal, but bear in mind that an appeal may result in
an even higher rent assessment.

Once a fair rent is registered, the landlord cannot raise
the rent for two years (three years in Scotland) unless
you and he apply to the Rent Officer together or there has
been a change of circumstances, such as major improvements to the property. At the end of two years, the
landlord can apply for a new registration.

In Northern Ireland, there are no rent officers. Instead,
there is a complex formula set down by law for deciding
in what circumstances rents can be raised.

If you are paying too much for services and repairs

If you pay a service charge to your landlord, you have the

right under the Housing Act 1985 to ask him for a summary of the costs on which the service charge is based and he must provide one. If you think that you should not have to pay for something in the summary, or that the cost is too high, tell the landlord or his managing agent. If this does not sort the problem out, you can take the landlord to the county court. The court will decide whether you should pay for the item and if so, whether the cost is reasonable.

If the tenants are liable for the cost of repairs and maintenance, the landlord must consult them before he carries out major maintenance or repair work. He must get at least two estimates for the work and at least one of these must be from a firm totally unconnected with him. He must then let the tenants know what these estimates are, although he does not actually have to take any notice of the tenants' views. If you think the cost of the work is too high you can take the landlord to court. The court will decide what is a reasonable charge. If the landlord starts work without consulting the tenants, they can either pay a limited amount (the limit per flat is laid down in law) and leave the landlord to sue them for the rest, or they can refuse to pay anything, take the landlord to court and let the court decide what is reasonable.

Getting help
If you have a housing problem, it is wise to seek expert help as soon as you can as the law is extremely complex. There are various places you can go for advice:

* Citizens' Advice Bureaux.

* Housing Aid Centres (listed in the telephone directory under that title); there are about 100 of these specialising in housing matters in towns and cities throughout the country.

* SHAC, the London Housing Aid Centre, operates a telephone enquiry line.

* Shelter can advise on all kinds of housing problems; it has offices in London and other cities.

* Law centres (listed in the telephone directory under that title).

* A solicitor specialising in landlord and tenant work. See Chapter 6 for how to find one.

11

Buying on Credit

You're unlikely to go through life without using credit. Even if you don't have a mortgage or a credit card and have never had a loan or bought on hire purchase, the chances are that you've let your bank account slip into the red once in a while or bought by instalments on mail order. If so, you have made use of credit. Leaving aside food, fuel and housing, one-third of consumer spending in this country is financed by credit.

Credit is a good friend and a bad enemy. Used wisely, it can take the waiting out of wanting – as the advertisements say – allowing you to shop now and pay later. It means you can buy today even if you do not have the cash, instead of hanging on and watching prices rise as you save.

Borrowing money is relatively easy: advertisements offering loans of one kind or another beckon from the pages of every newspaper, from street hoardings and from display counters in every bank; many shops offer easy terms when you buy large items. But of course you have to pay for this privilege and it is easy to over-commit yourself. The line between credit and debt is a fine one but, once crossed, that line can seem like a brick wall between you and solvency.

The Consumer Credit Act 1974 protects you when you buy on credit. It controls who can offer credit, the way they can advertise, the information they must give you before you sign, the procedure for ending a credit agreement, the steps a trader can take if you default, and almost every other aspect of almost every kind of credit transaction up to £15,000. It is intended to promote *truth in lending* and to ensure as far as possible that you know what is involved when you sign a credit deal and that you are treated fairly.

Different Kinds of Credit

From a bank

OVERDRAFTS

You go into the red on your current account up to a limit agreed with your bank manager (running up an overdraft *without* your bank manager's consent is a bad idea). It can be a cheap and flexible way of borrowing: you can spend the money how you like and are charged interest only on the amount by which you are overdrawn, not on your overdraft limit. However, you will pay more in bank charges if your account is overdrawn. The maximum you can borrow is decided by the bank manager (he may refuse you an overdraft completely) and the bank can ask you to pay the loan back at any point.

ORDINARY LOANS

You agree with your bank manager how much you want to borrow and for what purpose and arrange a repayment plan by instalments over a fixed period. The interest rate may fluctuate.

PERSONAL LOANS

These work in a similar way to ordinary loans except that the rate of interest is fixed. They generally cost more, but knowing exactly what the repayments will be should help you to budget.

BUDGET ACCOUNTS

These help you spread the burden of your bills over the year. You calculate what you're likely to spend annually on things like insurance, fuel, car servicing and holidays, and divide that by 12. Each month that figure is transferred by standing order from your current account to your budget account. It helps you budget but it can work out expensive because of the interest charges you pay when the account is overdrawn.

From a shop
Shops can arrange various kinds of credit, usually through finance companies. It is with the finance company that you actually make the agreement.

INTEREST-FREE CREDIT
You pay a deposit and then pay off the rest of the cost of the goods by monthly instalments at no interest. Make sure that the price you are paying for the goods is competitive compared with other shops.

HIRE PURCHASE OR CONDITIONAL SALE
This is a loan arranged to tie in with a particular purchase. You pay a deposit, take the goods and repay the rest by instalments. A hire purchase agreement must show clearly the cash price, the total hire purchase price, and the amount of each instalment. You do not own the goods until the last instalment is paid and therefore cannot sell them before then. Once you have paid more than a third of the total price, the finance company cannot repossess the goods without obtaining a court order.

CREDIT SALES
These work in a similar way to hire purchase except that the goods become yours as soon as you have paid the deposit. If you default on the payments the finance company cannot repossess the goods but must sue you for what you owe.

BUDGET ACCOUNTS
You agree to pay a minimum amount each month and you can then buy goods worth a multiple of that amount – say 24 times what you pay in each month. If

you spend more than is in your account you pay interest, but if you are in credit very few shops will pay *you* interest, so this can be an expensive way of borrowing.

MONTHLY ACCOUNTS
You can buy goods up to a pre-arranged limit, but you must pay off what you owe when the statement arrives each month.

OPTION ACCOUNTS
These work like monthly accounts except that you can settle all or part of your debt and are charged interest on what you owe. Interest rates are sometimes higher than for credit cards but they can be useful if you shop regularly at a place which doesn't take other cards.

From a finance company

PERSONAL LOANS
You will sometimes be offered a personal loan by a trader if you want to stagger the payments on a major item of expenditure, such as a car, double glazing or a new kitchen; or a finance company may advertise personal loans direct to the public. Make sure the firm you use is reputable and check the cost. It may be cheaper to approach your bank.

From an insurance company
If you have a life insurance policy with a cash-in value, the insurance company may lend you money against it. You pay interest on the loan at a fairly low rate and do not have to repay the sum you have borrowed until the policy ends, though of course you can repay it before if you prefer.

By credit card

BANK CREDIT CARDS
Although the two biggest credit cards in this country

are issued by banks, you do not have to have an account with the issuing bank in order to get one. You can spend up to your credit limit at any outlet which accepts your card. Each month you receive a statement listing your purchases and what you owe. You must pay off a minimum amount and, if you settle the statement in full before the payment date, you'll be charged no interest. If you play your cards right, you can have interest-free credit for up to eight weeks. But if you don't pay in full, you will be charged interest on what you owe at a fairly high rate. If you lose your credit card, telephone the card company immediately and follow your call up with a letter. If your card is stolen or lost, the Consumer Credit Act says that the maximum you will have to pay for purchases made by somebody else without your permission is £50 and you do not have to pay at all for purchases made after you reported the loss to the card company. It is a good idea to check regularly that you have not lost any of your credit cards. You should also check your statements for mistakes. Keep all your statements, and note on them how and when you settled the account.

CHARGE CARDS

You have to pay for a charge card and you must settle the full amount you owe each month. If you don't, you will be charged interest. If you consistently fail to pay on time, your card may be withdrawn. You have no spending limit.

GOLD CARDS

These are available only to people on high incomes. They work like charge cards but bring extra perks such as a guaranteed overdraft at a lower rate of interest. You can use them as cheque guarantee cards to withdraw large amounts from certain banks.

Check trading

A check trading company issues checks of different values and arranges for local shops to accept these in payment for goods. You usually buy the checks from the company and pay the check trader back in weekly instalments, with interest, which he collects from you at home. This can be an expensive way of borrowing.

From a mail order catalogue
Mail order catalogues allow you to spread the cost of your purchases over a number of instalments. There is not usually an extra charge for this, but the price of the goods may be higher than in some shops, so it is wise to compare. You may have to pay interest if you want to spread the payments over a longer period than usual – catalogues contain details of the charges made.

From a moneylender
This is an expensive way of borrowing. Moneylenders tend to be used by people who cannot get a loan elsewhere: the risk to the lender is high and so, therefore, are his interest rates. A moneylender is breaking the law if he:

- does not have a licence from the Office of Fair Trading; a credit agreement made by an unlicensed moneylender may not be enforceable
- takes your supplementary benefit or family allowance book as security or to obtain repayment of a loan
- calls on you to offer a loan without having a written invitation from you
- tries to recover a loan from you by using harassment.

See below (page 220) for what to do if you think you are being charged an extortionate rate for credit. If you think you are being unfairly treated by a moneylender in any way, contact the trading standards or consumer protection department at your local council offices.

From a pawnbroker
You hand the pawnbroker something of value and he lends you a sum of money on which he charges you interest, using your 'pledge' as security. If you do not

pay off the loan within the agreed time, the pawn-broker can sell the pledge. If he raises more from the sale than you owe, he must pay you the difference. If he raises less, he can ask you to make up the shortfall, although you can challenge whether he got a reasonable price for the goods. Pawnbrokers must be licensed by the Office of Fair Trading. They must give you a pawn-receipt.

From a credit union
These are made up of people who live in the same area or work together or who belong to the same organisation. Members save regularly and can borrow at an agreed rate of interest from the fund which accumulates. Interest rates are usually low and minimum weekly payments into the fund small, which makes credit unions useful for people who might otherwise have difficulty in borrowing money. Before you join one, try to make sure it is well managed. The Association of British Credit Unions can give you information on the subject.

Before You Borrow
It is just as important to think carefully and to shop around before you choose a method of credit as it is when buying goods and services. In many ways it is even more essential. Tying yourself up in a credit deal you cannot really afford could have far more serious consequences than buying the wrong washing machine for your needs.

Before you do your shopping around, note down:

- how much you need to borrow
- how you are going to repay it
- what monthly instalments you could afford
- what you need the money for.

Next look at all the various methods of borrowing that are open to you. Before you make a decision, follow the 'buy-laws'. Consider:

☞ how long the loan is for

☞ what the *total* cost of the loan is with interest

☞ what the Annual Percentage Rate of Interest (APR) is (see below, page 218)

☞ what the repayments are

☞ whether there are any administration charges which will put up the cost

☞ how convenient the loan is to arrange and to repay

☞ whether you have to pay a deposit

☞ whether the interest rate is fixed or variable

☞ whether you can get tax relief on the loan

☞ whether you need to put up some security and, if so, what this involves

☞ whether you need to find a guarantor for your loan

☞ what happens if you repay the loan early – will you be charged for doing this and how much will you have to pay?

☞ whether the lender is reputable

☞ what happens if you cannot afford the repayments – should you take out insurance to cover this possibility?

☞ whether there is a cooling-off period in which you can change your mind.

Bear in mind *all* these points before you make a decision. Don't let yourself be influenced too much by one particular feature of a loan – for example, the fact that it is offered by the shop where you are buying the goods and is therefore convenient.

Simon Simple saw a stereo unit reduced by £30 in a
sale at a local store. He could not afford to pay cash,
so he asked the store about their credit terms. They
offered hire purchase over two years and Simon
signed. Glancing at the HP agreement, he noticed
that the APR was 40 per cent and the total cost of the
credit was £120. The following day he saw the same
stereo in the window of another store at the full
price. He was just congratulating himself on
having found a bargain when he noticed that the
shop was offering easy-payment terms over two
years at an APR of 21 per cent. Simon asked for a
quotation and discovered to his shame that he
would have saved himself about £20 by buying in
the second shop, despite the fact that their basic
price for the stereo was higher.

Always read a credit agreement through carefully. By
law any credit agreement must tell you the name and
address of the lender, the APR (see below), what the
repayments are and when they are due. Credit agreements for a fixed term must also tell you the total charge
for the credit and the total amount payable. As well
as these basics you should make sure you know the
answers to all the points listed above before you sign.
Don't be tempted to skip the 'small print'. If there is
anything you do not understand, ask. If you are not
happy with the answers, ask for time to think about
it and consult a Citizens' Advice Bureau, Consumer
Advice Centre or Money Advice Centre. Never let
yourself be pressured into signing a credit agreement.

If you sign a credit agreement at home you may be
able to cancel it if you change your mind (see below,
page 220). But it is unwise to rely on this 'escape route'.

After You've Signed a Credit Agreement

* Keep all the documentation relating to the agreement
  in one, safe place.

* Keep a note of when and how you paid off the loan. If you pay by cheque or giro, keep the counterfoils and statements.

* If you write to the lender, keep copies of the correspondence.

The Annual Percentage Rate (APR)
To help you compare different credit deals, lenders must tell you the Annual Percentage Rate of charge (APR) when they give you a written quotation for credit. The APR is calculated in a precise way laid down by law and takes into account not only the interest but all the other charges made for providing credit and how and when the loan has to be repaid. Basically, the lower the APR, the better the credit deal.

If You Cannot Get Credit
When you apply to borrow money, the lender needs to know that you can afford to repay the debt. There are various methods he can use to help him make an assessment.

CREDIT SCORING
You fill in an application form and the lender gives you points for each piece of information. The points system is based on his past experience of good and bad payers. If you gain more than the 'pass' mark, you will get your loan; if you 'fail' you won't. There is no arguing with a 'fail' score but don't give up completely because different companies have different credit scoring methods.

CREDIT REFERENCE AGENCIES
These keep files on people's financial standing and what their record is like in paying off debts. If you are refused credit, ask the lender whether he has used a credit reference agency. When you apply for credit, you have the right to know the name and address of any agency consulted about you. The lender must give you this information provided you ask for it in writing

- you must take care of any goods you have already received either until you send them back or they are collected by the trader
- any deposit you have paid must be returned to you
- any agreements which are linked to the credit arrangement are also cancelled.

While his wife was out one evening, Simon Simple ordered a fitted kitchen from a salesman who called at his home. The salesman arranged a loan for Simon with a finance company. He also suggested an insurance policy which would cover the repayments should Simon be unable to meet them because of illness or redundancy. When Mrs Simple returned she told Simon they could not afford a new kitchen and she did not like the one he had chosen anyway. Because the credit agreement had been signed at home, Simon was entitled to cancel it. The purchase of the units and the insurance policy could also be cancelled because they were linked to the agreement.

You can cancel even if you have already received the loan, but you should repay the money within a month or before the first instalment is due. If you do so you will not have to pay any interest.

Some lenders may allow you a cooling-off period even when they are not obliged to do so by law. It is worth enquiring about this before you sign.

When You Buy Faulty Goods on Credit

As we have seen, you have certain rights against the supplier if goods or services you have bought turn out to be faulty or if the supplier has made a false statement of fact about them (see Chapter 3). When you buy on credit you may also have a claim against the lender. This applies if:

- what you bought cost between £100 and £30,000
- the loan was for no more than £15,000

- there is a connection between the lender and the supplier of the goods.

  This protection can also be useful if you have paid for something which does not materialise.

  It applies if a doorstep salesman arranges a personal loan to help you buy his products or a shop offers you a loan through a finance company to enable you to pay by instalments. It applies to check trading and to purchases by credit card if your card was first taken out after 1 July 1977 (when this part of the Consumer Credit Act came into operation). You may get less protection if your credit card was first taken out before this date, but it is worth approaching the card company to see if they are willing to help.

  You would not have a claim against the lender if:

- you arranged the loan yourself without the trader being involved; this would be the case if you took out a bank loan to pay for a car
- you used your credit card to withdraw cash to pay for the goods or services
- you used a charge card where you had to settle the bill *in full* each month when the statement arrived.

---

* If you are unhappy about goods or services you have paid for by credit, try settling the problem with the trader first.

---

* If you have no success, or if the trader has gone out of business, explain the problem to the finance or credit card company, enclosing copies of your correspondence with the trader. If you paid by credit card and have not yet settled up with the card company for that particular item, you *could* withhold payment, but you may be charged interest. If paying by instalments, do not stop the repayments or you could be in trouble for breach of contract.

---

* If you are not happy with the response you receive from the finance company, seek advice from a Consumer Advice or Money Advice Centre, a Citizens' Advice Bureau, or the trading standards or consumer protection department at your local council offices.

Alec Smart bought a set of garden furniture – four chairs and a table – costing £115 from a high street shop. He paid by credit card. Within a month, the arms of two chairs fell off. When Alec went to complain, he found the shop had closed down. He wrote to the credit card company, asking for a refund. After a long delay, the company wrote back offering Alec £40 compensation for the two chairs. Alec decided to accept.

When you buy something on hire purchase, con-ditional sale or credit sale, your rights in law when something goes wrong are against the *lender* only. In practice, you should approach the trader first.

Ending a Credit Agreement

If you think there is a possibility – short of winning the Pools – that you will be able to repay the loan early, find out what charges and interest will be levied. Under the Consumer Credit Act, you have the right to settle early and in most cases you are entitled to a rebate of some of the interest and charges you would have had to pay if the loan had run its course. There is a formula set out under the Consumer Credit Act for calculating the amount of the rebate.

This applies to all credit agreements, including hire purchase. But, if you want to *end* a hire purchase agreement by stopping the repayments and returning the goods – because you cannot afford to continue with it – you must have paid at least half of the total amount payable (unless of course the agreement specifies a smaller sum). If your instalment payments do not add up to half the total cost, you have to make up the extra before you can cancel the agreement and return the goods. Any arrears must be paid off before you can end the agreement. If you have damaged the goods, you may have to pay more than half the total cost. It is a good idea to seek advice if this is the case.

If You Cannot Pay

When you borrow money, you should consider taking out an insurance policy which would pay off what you owed if you were unable to work for some reason. You should also read the agreement carefully to see what rights the lender has if you cannot meet the repayments.

If you do default on your repayments, the lender must send you a notice outlining what you have done wrong, telling you what you must do to put matters right and giving you at least seven days in which to do it. The notice must also explain what will happen if you do not settle your liability within that time. You can apply for a court order allowing you more time to pay.

If you are buying goods on hire purchase and fall behind with the repayments, the lender has the right to repossess the goods. He needs a court order or your agreement before he can do this if:

- you have paid at least a third of the total amount payable, or
- he wants to enter your home to take the goods back.

If he tries to recover the goods without obtaining a court order, the agreement is at an end and you can claim back all you have paid.

If you cannot repay what you have borrowed:

---

* **don't** sweep the problem under the carpet. Debts don't diminish if they are ignored – they multiply. Contact the people to whom you owe money and explain your problems: they cannot help you if they do not know what is wrong. You may be able to reschedule the loan so the repayments are smaller.

---

* **don't** borrow more money to pay off what you owe without expert advice.

---

* **find out** if you are entitled to any state benefits or to rent and rate rebates.

---

* **find out** if you can get a tax rebate.

---

* **seek help** (see below).

If the person to whom you owe money is harassing you, he may be committing a criminal offence. Criminal harassment takes many forms, from making repeated calls about the matter to your workplace to pretending to be a policeman authorised to collect the debt. If you are being harassed, tell the police and the trading standards or consumer protection department at your local council offices. If the lender belongs to a creditors' trade association, tell the association too. It may take disciplinary action.

Getting Help

If you have a problem involving credit, try sorting it out first with the lender. If this fails, contact a Consumer Advice or Money Advice Centre, a Citizens' Advice Bureau, the trading standards or consumer protection department at your local council offices or a solicitor specialising in consumer credit problems.

There is a growing awareness that people who have run into financial difficulties need specialist professional help and it is the role of debt counsellors to provide this. Some debt counsellors work for local authorities, others at CABs or in Money Advice Centres. Unfortunately, the service is patchy and in some parts of the country there is no provision at all. To find out if there is a debt counselling service in your area, contact your nearest Citizens' Advice Bureau.

For more detailed advice on money problems, see *How to Cope with Credit and Deal with Debt*, by Ann Andrews and Peter Houghton (Allen & Unwin, London, 1986).

Complaints about Credit

* If you have a complaint about a **lender,** try to sort the problem out with the branch or office where the loan was granted.

* If you have no success, write to the organisation's chairman or managing director at the head office giving

all the relevant information about your loan and explaining why you are dissatisfied.

* If you still do not receive a satisfactory response, contact a CAB or Money Advice Centre or the trading standards or consumer protection department at your local council offices.

* If trading standards officers suspect that the lender is in breach of the Consumer Credit Act or is trading unfairly in some way, they may pass this information on to the Office of Fair Trading which is responsible for granting and renewing credit licences.

If you have a problem concerning **banking services**, including bank credit cards, the Banking Ombudsman may be able to help. All the major banks belong to the Ombudsman scheme. The Ombudsman will not intervene until you have exhausted the bank's own complaints procedure. This means starting with your local branch and finishing up with a letter to the Customer Relations Department or the chairman at head office. If this brings no success, write to the Banking Ombudsman who will advise you whether he can investigate your case. The Ombudsman's decision is binding on the bank, but if you are still dissatisfied, you can take legal action. Consult a solicitor before you consider going to court.

12

Insurance

Nobody enjoys spending money on insurance: choosing insurance is no fun, you end up with nothing to show for your cash except a piece of paper and you positively do *not* want your policy to give you value for money – in the sense that you hope you will never have to claim back what you have paid in. For these reasons and others, you probably take less care and time selecting your insurance policies than you do choosing the things it is supposed to cover – your home, your car, your belongings.

Most people only discover exactly what their policy says when they come to make a claim – and by then it may be too late. Do you know, for example, whether you would be covered if you accidentally smashed a cut-glass vase? (Answer: only if you had accidental damage cover.) Or how much your insurance company would pay for alternative accommodation if your home burnt down? (Answer: probably about 10 per cent of the sum you're insured for.) Or what would happen if thieves stole the colour television you had borrowed from a friend for a fortnight? (Answer: you would not normally be covered on your policy.)

You should shop around for insurance as you do for other commodities. And you should make very sure that you know what you are getting before you buy.

Who Sells Insurance

You can buy insurance from an insurance company
direct, through a registered insurance broker or
through an insurance agent. Some agents are full-time
while others are professionals such as solicitors, estate
agents or accountants who offer insurance as an extension of their other services.

Obviously, if you deal directly with an **insurance
company,** you will only be offered *its* policies. The
advantage of buying direct is that the person you deal
with is likely to be very familiar with his company's
policies; so there should be less risk of misunderstandings occurring. But you won't save yourself any money:
although the company avoids having to pay commission to a broker or other intermediary, it does not pass
that saving on to you.

If you buy from an intermediary, you will give yourself extra protection by sticking to **registered insurance
brokers.** By law, nobody can call themselves an insurance broker unless they and their firm are registered
with the Insurance Brokers' Registration Council.
Registered brokers must:

---

* act with 'utmost good faith and integrity' and 'place the
interests of their clients before all other considerations'

---

* keep their clients' money in a separate bank account

---

* have professional indemnity insurance which will pay
out if a client loses money as a result of negligence by
the broker

---

* adhere to a Code of Conduct, which says, among other
things, that the broker will:

  • explain, if you ask, the differences between the
    various types of insurance policy which he thinks
    will suit your needs and compare costs for you
  • deal with a range of insurers and offer a wide choice
    of policies
  • tell you, if asked, how much commission he will

receive for any policy you are considering taking
out through him

- tell you of any charges that you will have to pay,
over and above the premium.

If you are worried that your broker is merely recommending the policy which earns him the biggest commission, you can ask him to disclose what he would
earn on other similar policies – you may find it doesn't
vary much. Still in doubt? Then contact other brokers to
see what they have to offer. Most insurance brokers
belong to the British Insurance Brokers' Association,
which can supply the names and addresses of members
in your area.

All the major banks run insurance broking operations. If your local manager cannot answer your
questions, he can arrange for an insurance expert to
meet you.

Once the Financial Services Act 1986 comes into force
in 1987, anybody who sells investments as defined in
the Act, including investment-type life assurance, will
have to be **authorised.** This means that they are judged
by one of the regulatory organisations to be 'fit and
proper' people to do business and are bound by certain
rules covering the way they deal with their customers.
If they misbehave, they can be disciplined. Selling
investment-type life assurance without authorisation
will be a criminal offence. See below (pages 241–3) for
more detail on life assurance.

If you go to an insurance agent or consultant who is
not a broker and who is not authorised under the
Financial Services Act, you have no guarantee that he is
reputable (unless of course he is a professional such as a
solicitor or accountant who is bound by the rules of his
own organisation). In theory, he could have come out of
prison the day before after serving five years for fraud
and extortion. Of course, many agents are highly competent and reliable; choose one who is well-established
and has been recommended to you.

All insurance companies that belong to the Association of British Insurers have agreed to ensure that
anybody (apart from registered brokers, who have

their own code) who sells their policies will adhere to
a Code of Practice covering their dealings with customers. Among other things this says that the salesman or
intermediary will:

- identify himself to you, make it clear that he will want
  to discuss insurance with you and say whether he is an
  agent for one or several insurance companies
- ensure as far as possible that the policy he recommends
  meets your needs
- explain the essential features of the cover provided by
  any policy he is recommending so that you understand
  what you are buying
- draw attention to any restrictions or exclusions in the
  policy
- tell you if there are any charges to pay over and above
  the premium.

Choosing Insurance

There is insurance available to cover every possession
and every contingency. Each category of insurance has
its own ground rules and below I look at the types you
are most likely to need and point out the main features
and problem areas. But there are some basic 'buy-laws'
you should follow before you choose any kind of policy.

☞ Decide before you do your shopping around what type
of cover you want and whether you want it to include
any special features.

☞ Get a few quotes from different companies or ask a
broker or agent to do this for you. If you have not used a
broker or agent before, approach a few to see what they
come up with.

☞ Do not choose an insurance policy solely on price. With
insurance, as with everything else, you do – to some
extent anyway – get what you pay for. If one policy is
much cheaper than another, find out why: it may offer
slightly different cover.

☞ Once you have found a policy which seems to suit you, **read it carefully.** This may be extremely tedious but it is essential. Following pressure from consumers, some policy documents are now written in simple English. But many are not. If there is anything you do not understand, ask the intermediary with whom you are dealing to explain, or approach the company yourself.

☞ Ask about the main exclusions to the policy as well as what *is* covered.

☞ Find out whether the policy has an 'excess' – in other words whether you have to pay anything towards the cost of any claim.

☞ Try to find out what kind of a reputation the company has for settling claims. How fast are they – and how fair?

☞ Find out whether the company belongs to the Insurance Ombudsman Bureau or the Personal Insurance Arbitration Service. You may want to use the services of the IOB or PIAS if you have a complaint about the company which you cannot resolve (see below, page 246).

☞ Do not let yourself be talked into taking out insurance of any kind if you are uncertain whether it is right for you or whether you can afford it. Think carefully before you sign.

☞ If a salesman or intermediary fills out the proposal form, read it through carefully before you sign. If the information given on your behalf is wrong, the company may refuse to meet your claim.

Household Insurance – Buildings

What it covers
Buildings insurance normally covers:

- the structure of your home
- fixtures and fittings such as built-in cupboards, baths and sinks
- interior decoration
- garages, greenhouses and sheds
- walls, fences, gates, paths, drives and swimming pools

Against damage by:

- fire, lightning, explosion, earthquake
- thieves, vandals, riots
- storm and flood
- impact from vehicles or animals or things falling from aircraft
- subsidence, heave or landslip
- water escaping from tanks and pipes and oil escaping from fixed heating systems.

You will also be covered for the cost of:

- alternative accommodation if your home is so badly damaged by one of the above happening that you cannot live in it
- accidental damage to underground pipes and cables supplying your home
- breakage of baths, toilets, sinks and glass in windows and doors.

What it does not cover

- The policy will probably *not* cover damage to gates and fences by storm or flood, or the cost of repairing pipes and tanks that leak.
- Cracks in your home caused by settlement – as opposed to subsidence – may also be excluded.
- You may not be covered for some kinds of damage if your house is empty for more than a certain time – typically 30 days.
- You should not expect your policy to cover wear and tear to your property. You may notice that your roof leaks during a storm, but if the storm did not actually

cause the leak, the insurers are not obliged to pay for
your ruined decorations.

Which company?

If you have a mortgage, your bank or building society
will probably suggest which company should insure
your property. You do not have to accept their suggestion and indeed it is a good idea to shop around before
you choose, as you may be able to find a better deal.

For how much?

When you decide how much to insure your home for,
you should base your calculations on what it would
cost to rebuild it completely and not on its market
value. Include fixtures and fittings and outbuildings
in your estimate, together with demolition costs and
architects' and surveyors' fees.

It is dangerous to underestimate. For one thing, your
insurers will not provide enough money for you to
rebuild your home to its previous standard if it is
destroyed. What is more, you may be penalised on *any*
claim you make because the insurance company may
apply the principle known as 'average'. This means
that if you insure your home for £25,000 when it would
actually cost twice that to rebuild, the company may
meet only half of any claim you make. So if a pipe burst
causing £500 worth of damage to your decorations, the
company might pay only £250.

To find out the total cost of rebuilding your home you
can:

* call in an architect or surveyor
* use the valuation given by the bank or building society
  with which you have a mortgage
* make your own estimate using the leaflet 'Buildings
  Insurance for Home Owners', published by the
  Association of British Insurers.

Rebuilding costs rise each year. To make sure that the
sum your home is insured for stays in line with infla-

tion, you should have a policy which is index-linked. If you improve your home in a way which would affect the cost of rebuilding – by installing double glazing, say, or adding a loft-room – then you should tell the insurance company.

Household Insurance – Contents

Choosing contents insurance is more complicated because there are more options open to you. This makes it even more important to do your homework beforehand. One survey of people whose claims under their contents insurance were not settled in full by their insurers showed that a quarter of them had claimed for a loss which was simply not covered under their policy!

What it covers

Contents insurance usually covers your movable belongings against loss or damage, while they are in your home, from:

- fire, lightning, explosion or earthquake
- thieves, vandals, riots
- storm and flood
- subsidence, heave or landslip
- impact by vehicles or animals or things falling from aircraft
- falling trees or aerials
- water escaping from tanks and pipes and oil escaping from fixed heating systems

You will usually also be covered for:

- the cost of alternative accommodation if your home is so badly damaged by one of the above happening, that you cannot live in it
- breakage of mirrors and glass in furniture
- personal and occupier's liability. This means your insurers would pay out up to a certain amount if you were found to be legally responsible for injury to somebody else or damage to their property. This might arise if a

friend tripped on a crack in your garden path and broke his leg or if you stepped in front of a cyclist causing him to fall off his bike and fracture his wrist.

There are two kinds of contents cover:

- with **indemnity,** a deduction is made for wear and tear;
- with **new-for-old,** you receive enough to replace what you have lost with a brand new item.

Some items such as clothes and linens and belongings over a certain age will often be covered on an indemnity basis even in a new-for-old policy. Check what yours says. New-for-old obviously costs more but gives you better cover. Some policies allow you to insure some items on a new-for-old basis and others with indemnity cover.

> Alec Smart decided to go for new-for-old cover, even though the premiums were higher. He was glad he did. When thieves stole his four-year-old video recorder, he was able to replace it with a new one of the same make. If he had had indemnity cover, the company would have knocked off quite a bit for wear and tear and he would only have been paid enough to buy a second-hand or a cheaper machine.

Extra cover
You can buy more extensive cover than this, but it will cost you more.

* You can, for example, cover your belongings against **accidental damage.** This would protect you if you dropped a cup of coffee on your cream carpet or if cigarette ash burned a hole in your settee.

* You can insure all your belongings on an **all-risks**

basis. All risks policies are expensive and give you a high level of cover, but even they have some exclusions.

* If you do not have an all-risks policy – and most people don't – you should insure belongings which you are likely to take out of the house with you such as cameras, watches and jewellery under an **all-risks extension** to your contents policy. Particularly valuable items should also be included in the all-risks section. But the fact that something is covered by an all-risks extension does not mean you can afford to be careless. It is a condition of most household policies that you will take reasonable steps to prevent loss or damage to your property. So if you leave a fur coat draped across the back seat of your car or your handbag on the floor of a shop while you wander off to try on clothes, your insurers may refuse to pay out if they are stolen.

What it does not cover

- If you have lent or let your house you will not normally be covered for theft unless there has been a forced entry.
- Damage from sonic bangs is not usually included.
- There may be exclusions if the house is empty for more than a certain time – typically 30 days.
- Borrowed goods aren't covered.
- Once again, you cannot expect your policy to cover normal wear and tear.
- If your company insists that you have any special security devices fitted, such as a burglar alarm or window locks, it will expect you to use them. If you don't and you are burgled, it may refuse to meet your claim.

Which company?

There can be very wide variations in the cost of contents insurance and it is worth getting a number of quotes. What you pay depends not only on the cover you choose and the sum you insure for, but also on where you live; and companies do have different ideas about what they consider to be high-risk areas. Before you plump for the lowest quote, make sure that it gives you the cover you want and that there are no strings attached.

For how much?
Go from room to room working out what it would cost to replace **everything you own** at today's prices. For any items insured on an indemnity basis, you can knock off something for wear and tear. How much depends on the age of the item and how long it would normally be expected to last. Television sets, for example, are reckoned to last about ten years. If yours is five years old, it is estimated to be worth half the price of a new model.

Because the cost of replacing your belongings will go up each year, you should make sure you are insured for the right amount. If your policy is **index-linked,** the sum you are insured for automatically rises in line with inflation. As with buildings insurance, the insurers may apply the principle of 'average' if you are under-insured.

Simon Simple was astonished to find, when he added up the replacement value of his belongings, that it came to £20,000 and that he would have to pay £200 a year in insurance premiums. He thought he would save himself some money by insuring the contents of his home for only £10,000 instead. When he was burgled, Simon claimed the cost of replacing the stolen items – about £2,000. But the insurance company soon discovered he had under-insured and – applying 'average' – paid out only half what he had claimed.

Motor Insurance

What it covers
Exactly what is covered by your motor insurance depends on the type of policy you have.

- **Road Traffic Act** is the lowest level of cover allowed by law. It covers you for injuries to other people only. Very few people have such limited cover.

- **Third Party** gives you the same cover as above plus cover for damage to other people's cars and property.

- **Third Party, Fire and Theft** gives you the same cover as above plus cover if your car is stolen or damaged by fire.

- **Fully Comprehensive** gives you the same cover as above, plus the cost of repairing damage to your car up to its value at the time of the accident and the theft of items from inside your car up to a maximum amount.

Extra cover

- If you make a claim – even if the accident was not your fault – you will lose your no claims discount. Some companies offer policies which protect your discount even if you make a claim; obviously you pay extra for this protection.
- You can also insure your windscreen separately, so that if it is smashed by a stone and you need to claim for a replacement you will not jeopardise your no claims discount. If you have comprehensive cover this kind of windscreen insurance may be automatically included.
- Some policies reimburse you for the cost of hiring another car while yours is being repaired.

What it does not cover

- Your insurers will want to know whether you are using

the car for domestic or business purposes or both. You will only be covered while using it for the purposes which you have declared.

● If you drive another car you will usually be covered on your own policy but you will have only third party protection. It is therefore a good idea to make sure you are covered to drive under the owner's policy and that this is comprehensive. Other drivers named on your policy are not covered at all under your policy when they drive other cars.

● If you let somebody else drive *your* car, make sure your policy covers this. If it does not, check whether *his* policy allows him to drive a borrowed car. If it does, he will have third party cover only while driving your car. If it does not – and he is not insured under your policy – you and he are breaking the law.

What it costs
Unlike household insurance, where the cost depends mainly on the sum insured and the type of cover you have, the cost of car insurance is determined by a host of factors including:

* the type of car
* where you live
* your age and occupation
* your driving experience and record
* what the car is used for
* how many drivers are named on the policy, their ages and driving records
* the type of cover you want
* the size of your no claims discount.

Warning!
☞ Do not be tempted to reduce the size of your premiums by 'twisting the truth' when you apply for insurance. If the insurers find out – as they are quite likely to if you make a claim – they may refuse to pay out.

Simon Simple bought his daughter an old banger to take to college with her. He was shocked when his insurance company quoted more for insuring the car than it actually cost. To save money, Simon insured it 'in his name', thus halving the cost of the premium. Unfortunately, his daughter drove into the back of another car outside college. His insurers investigated the claim, discovered the truth and 'avoided the policy', which meant Simon had to meet the cost of damage to both cars out of his own pocket.

No claims discounts

Unless you have a policy which protects your no claims discount, you will lose your discount (even if the accident was entirely somebody else's fault) if you make a claim and your insurers cannot get back from the other driver or his insurers all they pay out. This may arise:

* if you are at least partly to blame for the accident

* if you cannot prove that you were not to blame – because there were no independent witnesses, say, and the other driver disagrees with your version of events

* if you cannot trace the other driver

* if you fill in an accident report form for your insurers – as your policy says you must – and do not make it clear that you do not wish to make a claim

* if the claim is settled on a knock-for-knock basis between the two insurers, with each company paying for the damage to the car it has insured, regardless of blame. This arrangement *should* have no bearing on what happens to your no claims discount but, unless you can provide some evidence that the other driver

admits liability for the accident, you may lose your discount.

Life Assurance

What it covers
There are three main kinds of life assurance:

- With **term assurance** you pay in for a certain length of time and your insurers pay out if you die within that time. This is the cheapest kind of life insurance and can be used to cover you for a period in your life when your death would be particularly disastrous financially for your family, or those who work with you. It is often used as a 'mortgage protection' policy.

- With **whole life assurance** you pay in every year until you retire or until you die and your insurers pay out whenever you die.

- With **endowment assurance** you pay in for an agreed period – say 20 years – and your insurers pay out either when the agreed period is up or when you die, whichever is the sooner.

Some policies are **convertible,** which means that they can be changed to a different type of policy without your having to go through the formalities – including a medical examination – again. This might be useful if you could afford only a term policy initially but hoped to be able to afford a higher level of cover later.

If you have whole life or endowment assurance, you can pay extra to have a **with profits** policy. This means that the company pays you a bonus as well as the sum you have assured. The size of the bonus depends on what profit the company has made on its investments over the years.

A **unit-linked** policy should also bring you extra benefits. In this case much of your premium is connected with particular investments which the company makes and what you finally receive depends on how well these investments are performing at the time the benefit is paid to you – unit values can go down as well as up.

As the amount of money you receive from a with-profits or unit-linked policy depends on how success-ful the company is at investing its money, you should do some careful research before you take out a policy of this kind. Find out about the company's past perform-ance, but do not be swept away by the promise of what might seem to be colossal sums.

Remember!
☞ Inflation bites deep. Thirty years ago you could buy a house for £1,500; today many people spend that on a family holiday.

Buying life assurance
There are so many different kinds of life assurance on the market and so many salesmen competing for com-mission that choosing the right policy for your needs can be a complex task. The law and the insurance industry between them give you valuable protection in this area. The Financial Services Act, which comes into force in 1987, says that anybody authorised to sell investment-type life assurance must:

- deal honestly and fairly with their customers
- take reasonable steps to find out what your personal circumstances are before advising you or making recommendations
- recommend only policies that they genuinely believe are suitable for you
- act with due care, skill and diligence.

The organisations supervising life assurance market-ing will draw up detailed rules covering the way life assurance is sold. These are expected to say that:

- Company representatives should recommend what they genuinely believe to be the best policy for you offered by their company.

- Independent intermediaries should take reasonable steps to seek out and recommend the most appropriate policy for you on the market.
- The salesman with whom you are dealing should tell you:

  – the nature of the policy being offered
  – what it will cost you
  – what the tax implications are
  – what the consequences are and what you are likely to get back if you stop paying the premiums and surrender the policy early
  – how much the policy may eventually pay out
  – either how much commission he is earning from the deal or whether his commission falls within the levels agreed by the industry. This applies only to independent intermediaries, not to company salesmen.

The Financial Services Act does not apply to *term assurance* because this is not an investment: the person taking out the policy does not receive any personal benefit as the policy pays out only after his death.

The law allows you to change your mind after you have bought most kinds of life assurance. The company must send you a notice telling you of your right to cancel within ten days (this will be extended to 14 days under the Financial Services Act). If you do so, any premium you have paid will be refunded.

The life assurance industry has a **code of practice** covering how life assurance should be sold and a **Statement of Long Term Insurance Practice** covering the way life assurance proposal forms and policies are worded and the way claims are treated (see below, page 244).

Proposal Forms – the Duty to Disclose
Whenever you apply for insurance, you will be asked to fill in a proposal form. This gives the insurance company the information it needs to assess whether to issue a policy and what premiums to charge. Proposal forms contain many specific questions and I have

already stressed the importance of answering these truthfully.

However, you also have a duty to disclose any other information that might be relevant in helping the company to decide whether or not to accept your proposal. The trouble is that it can be hard for you to know what is relevant and what is not. Clearly, the fact that you go hang-gliding every weekend would be considered a 'material fact' to anybody assessing you for life assurance. But if a proposal form for contents insurance asks no questions about previous convictions, should you reveal that you have been found guilty of shoplifting? At least one insurance company thinks you should.

The two Statements of Practice on Insurance Practice – one on general insurance and the other on long-term (i.e. life) insurance – which have been drawn up by the insurance industry, say that a company will refuse to meet a claim on the grounds of non-disclosure or mis-representation only if the material fact which you have not declared is one which you could reasonably have been expected to disclose.

The final decision on what is 'material' rests with the company – though if you disagree you can follow the complaints procedure described in the next section. If you are in doubt as to whether a fact is relevant or not, check with your insurance company. With insurance contracts that you renew each year – such as household and car insurance – you should let the company know about any changes in your circumstances which occur after you have filled out the proposal form.

Simon Simple decided to let his spare room to the daughter of a friend, who was studying at the local teacher training college. When his contents policy came up for renewal, he didn't tell his insurers about the change. Later in the year burglars squeezed through an open window and made off with all his wife's jewellery. When the insurance company discovered that Simon had a lodger they refused to meet his claim, pointing to a clause in the policy which said that cover for theft is excluded

when a house is in 'multiple occupancy' unless
there has been forced entry or exit.

How to Complain about Insurance

Insurance brokers

* If you have a complaint about an insurance broker who
  is a member of the British Insurance Brokers' Association you can ask BIBA's consumer relations officer to
  investigate.

* If this does not bring a solution, or the matter concerns
  serious professional misconduct by the broker, you
  should write to the Registrar of the Insurance Brokers'
  Registration Council.

Life assurance intermediaries

* If you have a complaint about an independent intermediary who has sold you life assurance, you should
  contact the Financial Intermediaries, Managers and
  Brokers Regulatory Association (FIMBRA).

* If, once the Financial Services Act is in force, you lose
  money owing to the fraud or insolvency of an authorised intermediary, you will be compensated.

Other intermediaries

* There is no supervision over intermediaries who are
  not brokers, do not belong to a professional body
  (such as the Law Society or the Institute of Chartered
  Accountants) and are not authorised under the Financial Services Act. If you have a complaint against one,
  which you cannot resolve, try contacting the insurance
  company that issued the policy. Failing that, you will

have to decide whether to take legal action against the intermediary.

Insurance companies
There is a series of steps to follow if you have a complaint about your insurance company:

* Discuss the matter with the manager at the office which issued the policy.

* Write to the chief executive at the company's head office giving all the relevant details of your policy and claim and outlining your complaint clearly and concisely.

* If the company is a member of the Association of British Insurers, contact the ABI's Consumer Information Department.

* If the company belongs to the Insurance Ombudsman Bureau, find out whether the Ombudsman can investigate your complaint. Even if he cannot, the Bureau may be able to offer you some useful advice on your problem. Its services are free.

* If the Ombudsman investigates your case and you disagree with his decision, you can take legal action against the company.

* If your company is not a member of the IOB, it may subscribe to the Personal Insurance Arbitration Service (PIAS) scheme run by the Chartered Institute of Arbitrators. Arbitration under the scheme is free but – unlike the decision of the Ombudsman – legally binding on you. So if you are unhappy with the arbitrator's decision, you cannot take your case to court.

Insurance companies must be authorised by the Department of Trade and Industry. If an authorised insurance company goes into liquidation, the Policyholders' Protection Act 1975 ensures that 90 per cent of any claim you are making at the time is met (100 per cent in the case of compulsory insurance such as third party motor insurance).

Lloyd's

* All Lloyd's policies are sold through insurance brokers, so the broker who arranged your insurance should be your first port of call.

* If he cannot solve the problem, write to the manager of the Consumer Enquiries Department at Lloyd's giving him the factual information he will need to investigate your case. He will discuss the matter with the under-writer who issued the policy.

* If you are not satisfied with the manager's decision, you should seek legal advice (see Chapter 13).

* Neither the IOB nor PIAS can at present deal with problems concerning Lloyd's, though this may change in the future.

13

Taking It Further

So far in this book I have looked at the main ways in which you are likely to spend your money, set out the steps you can take to make sure you get good value and explained what to do if things go wrong. The emphasis has been on how, as far as possible, to prevent problems and how to deal with them if they do arise. In each chapter, I have suggested where to go for further advice if you get nowhere on your own, but the emphasis has been very much on self-help.

Sometimes, however, your own skill and determination in presenting your complaint are not enough to get the problem sorted out. You meet a blank wall of denials, evasions or just plain indifference. At this point you have to decide whether to take the matter further – in other words, whether to start court proceedings, or to go to arbitration.

Getting Help

The main purpose of this chapter is to explain what legal action involves. However, before you take this step, it is a good idea to seek specialist advice. A consumer adviser may be able to use his professional expertise and contacts to settle the matter when you and the trader involved are at loggerheads. And if he does not succeed either, he will at least be able to tell you whether it is likely to be worth your taking further action, or whether you are simply wasting your time. Going to court or arbitration should be seen as a last resort – to be used when all else fails.

Citizens' Advice Bureaux

CABs offer information and advice on a vast range of subjects, including virtually all those dealt with in this book. They can give you basic information, write letters on your behalf, and may be able to help you prepare a case for court. If they cannot help you, they will be able to put you in touch with somebody who can. The service is free and confidential. There are 910 CABs throughout the country and you can find your nearest by looking under 'Citizens' Advice Bureau' in the telephone directory.

Consumer Advice Centres

CACs specialise in problems involving goods and services and can help you present your case, from negotiating with the trader to accompanying you to court (though not all CACs have sufficient staff to go to court). They are run by the local authority and staffed by paid consumer advisers. There are about 55 CACs, concentrated mainly in the major cities. To find out if there is one near you, contact the trading standards or consumer protection department at your local council offices.

Trading standards and consumer protection departments

Trading standards officers work for the local authority (in Northern Ireland for the Trading Standards Branch of the Department of Economic Development for Northern Ireland). It is their job to enforce the mass of criminal legislation which protects us when we buy goods and services. These are the people to turn to if you suspect the law has been broken: when you have been sold short measure at your local, or discover that your new car had done 50,000 miles instead of the 20,000 that were on the clock, or your new lawnmower gives you an electric shock. As well as enforcing the law, trading standards departments will give advice on consumer problems and tell you what steps to take.

Law centres

Staff at a law centre will give advice on consumer problems and may take a case to court on your behalf. They are principally for people who cannot afford to pay a solicitor's fees. There are 57 law centres in the country, concentrated in the major cities. To find out if there is one near you, ask at a Citizens' Advice Bureau.

Which? Personal Service

If you subscribe to *Which?* magazine, published by the Consumers' Association, you can pay an additional annual fee to join the Which? Personal Service. You are then entitled to free legal advice. The service will guide you through the whole process of getting your problem sorted out, helping you bring a case to court if necessary, and will take up your complaint with the trader on your behalf where appropriate.

Solicitors

All the organisations listed above can give you legal advice and some of them can put you in touch with a solicitor. However, you may prefer – or one of the above organisations may advise you – to see a solicitor privately. This might apply if your case involves much money or personal injury, or is especially complicated. See Chapter 6 (pages 115–20) for how to choose and use a solicitor.

Consumer organisations

There are a number of national organisations whose job it is to represent consumers' interests in dealings with government, industry and others. These bodies cannot investigate individual complaints. However, they can be of great benefit to consumers generally and it is worth outlining their different functions here.

The Office of Fair Trading is a government department which keeps an eye on trading practices and encourages competition in business. The Office encourages trade associations to draw up codes of practice, publishes useful leaflets on common consumer problems, investigates issues which concern consumers and, where appropriate, suggests changes in the law or in business practices. It also checks on firms and individuals who offer credit facilities and deals with traders who persistently break the law or treat their customers badly.

The National Consumer Council is a government-funded but independent body with particular responsibility for highlighting the problems of poor and disadvantaged consumers. It carries out research and produces reports on a wide range of topics from the need for Plain English in legal documents to the problems of council house tenants. Its campaigns have led to a number of changes in the law including the passing of the Supply of Goods and Services Act. The NCC has sister bodies doing similar work in Scotland and Wales.

The Consumers' Association publishes *Which?*, *Holiday Which?* and *Gardening Which?* The reports in these magazines are based on detailed independent testing and research into a wide range of goods and services. CA also publishes books on many consumer topics. It lobbies industry and government when it believes changes are needed to improve matters for consumers. Which? Personal Service gives legal advice to subscribers (see above).

The National Federation of Consumer Groups is the national body representing local member consumer groups all over Britain. It carries out research, and campaigns for changes in the law or business practices when it believes such changes would bring a better deal for consumers.

Taking Legal Action – Court or Arbitration?

When you have tried – and failed – to sort out your problem with the trader involved, his head office and his trade or professional association, when letters from you and your consumer advisers have drawn a blank, then you will have to decide whether to give up altogether or whether to take your case to court or to arbitration. You cannot normally do both, and you may not have a choice: sometimes you *have* to go to arbitration and sometimes you cannot choose arbitration even if you would prefer it.

Arbitration under Codes of Practice

There have been various references in this book to codes of practice drawn up by trade associations and other bodies, often with the backing of the Office of Fair Trading. These codes include informal complaints procedures for helping to settle disputes between traders and consumers. Some codes also feature an independent arbitration scheme which can be used if conciliation fails. This provides a legally binding method of resolving disputes which does not involve going to court. If you ask for arbitration under a code of practice, the trader must agree. There are code of practice arbitration schemes covering:

- cars
- motorcycles
- holidays
- domestic electrical appliance servicing
- double glazing
- photographic services
- catalogue mail order
- furniture
- funerals
- postal services

- telephone services
- rail services.

The Personal Insurance Arbitration Service (PIAS) and the Solicitors' Arbitration Scheme work in a similar way to the code of practice schemes.

Arbitration under codes of practice is intended to be simple, cheap, convenient and quick. You do not have to attend a hearing: instead, you and the trader send in any documents relevant to the case and the arbitrator makes his decision on the basis of these. Occasionally – for example if you are complaining about double glazing which does not fit – the arbitrator will visit your home to see for himself.

Arbitration under a code of practice may be a sensible choice if:

---

* you would prefer the whole matter to be dealt with on paper, rather than having to appear in court

---

* you do not have the time to prepare a case for court and attend a court hearing, possibly in another town

---

* you are claiming more than £500. At present this is the maximum you can claim under the small claims procedure in the county court if you want to avoid legal costs. A few code of practice arbitration schemes do have limits on the amount you can claim, but this is generally higher than £500.

Arbitration has two further advantages:

---

* If you win your case but the trader is reluctant to pay up, the trade association to which the trader belongs will put pressure on him and this is usually effective.

---

* The most you will have to pay if you lose is your own and the trader's registration fees.

Arbitration is probably not a good idea if:

---

* there is little documentation to support your case

* the matter turns on your word against the trader's. Generally speaking, the arbitrator is trying to discover whether the trader has fulfilled his contract with you. If everything was agreed verbally rather than in writing, the arbitrator has very little to go on and you would be wiser to present your case in court.

* you feel the case is too complex to explain fully on paper.

   Obviously you cannot go to arbitration if your dispute is with a trader who does not belong to one of the organisations which subscribe to an arbitration scheme.

Code of practice arbitration – step-by-step
The Office of Fair Trading publishes a useful booklet 'I'm Going to Take it Further', which explains how arbitration works and what types of complaint can be dealt with in this way. With one exception – the Motor Agents' Association scheme – all the arbitration schemes under codes of practice are run by the Chartered Institute of Arbitrators. Although the schemes are partly funded by the trade associations concerned, the arbitrators are independent. Below is a brief summary of the procedure for most schemes.

* After you have exhausted the other complaints procedures operated by the trade association concerned, ask the association for an application form and a copy of their code of practice. Read the code and the rules of the arbitration scheme carefully.

* Fill in the application form, giving brief details of the dispute.

* Return the application form to the trade association with the registration fee. The size of the fee depends on how much you are claiming: fees for most schemes start

at £17.25 for claims up to £2,500. If you win, the arbitrator can order the trader to pay your registration fee. If you lose, you may have to pay his. Once you have signed the registration form for arbitration, you cannot decide you would rather go to court.

* The Institute will send you a claim form. Explain clearly and in detail exactly what happened, with dates. Enclose two copies of anything that might help your case including photographs, witness statements, correspondence, invoices and receipts and keep your own copy of everything you send. You can submit an expert's report if you think it would be useful, but you will have to pay for this yourself – even if you win the case. The claim form must be returned to the Institute within 28 days.

* The trader will be sent a copy of your claim and he has 28 days in which to submit his defence.

* The arbitrator (called an arbiter in Scotland) will consider the evidence you and the trader have submitted and may ask either of you for more information. He may ask a technical expert to make a report.

* The arbitrator normally takes a few weeks to reach a decision. You and the trader will be told what the decision is and given the arbitrator's reasons.

* The arbitrator's decision is binding. You can appeal to a court only if the arbitrator has made a mistake on a point of law.

Compulsory Arbitration

Some contracts for services contain a clause saying that, if there is a dispute, you will go to arbitration rather than to court. Generally speaking you are bound by this clause, although you can start court proceedings. If the trader lodges a defence, thus agreeing to court proceedings, the case can be heard in court. In Scotland, if you sign a contract including a compulsory arbitration clause, you are bound by it.

Going to Court

To many people the idea of going to court is daunting. They fear that it will prove very costly, time-consuming and complicated. In fact, if you limit the size of your claim, it need be none of these things.

The small claims procedure

When you sue somebody for less than £5,000, your case is dealt with in a county court. When you are claiming more than £5,000, you must generally go to the High Court. Both these courts are **civil courts.** Law-breakers are dealt with in a different set of courts – the **criminal courts.**

If you are claiming £500 in money or less (£300 in Northern Ireland), your case will be dealt with under the small claims procedure. This is known as arbitration, but is quite different from the type of arbitration described above. The small claims procedure in the county court is not like a trial. The case is normally heard in a private room, rather than in open court. The hearing is usually less formal than a trial – though the exact form it takes depends on the registrar concerned – and is designed so that you can bring your own case without using a solicitor. There is nothing to stop either party using a solicitor but solicitors' costs are not normally awarded against the losing party. So, if you lose, there is no danger of your having to pay the other side's legal fees. Equally, if you are legally represented and you win, you will not be able to claim your solicitor's fees back. The no-costs rule is intended to discourage both sides from having legal representation.

The small claims procedure may be a sensible choice if:

* your claim is for £500 or less

* the trader does not belong to one of the organisations that have drawn up a code of practice with an arbitration scheme

* you want the opportunity to explain your case in person and to call witnesses.

However you should remember that:

* preparing a case for court does take time and effort

* there is no guarantee that you will get your money even if you win. **If you do not think the person you are considering suing has the means to pay – because he has gone out of business perhaps – there is absolutely no point in taking him to court. The same applies if you think you are dealing with a rogue who *will not* pay even though he has the money.** Enforcing judgment against somebody takes time and costs money (see below, pages 265–6).

If you lose, you may have to pay:

* the winning party's court fees
* his expenses in preparing the case and attending the hearing
* his witnesses' expenses
* any costs which the registrar decides the trader has incurred because you behaved unreasonably.

* there is no appeal unless the arbitrator has made a mistake on a point of law.

At the time of writing, a small claims procedure is being devised for Scotland. The precise details of the scheme have not been decided.

The small claims procedure – step-by-step
The booklet *Small Claims in the County Court*, published by the Lord Chancellor's Department and available from Citizens' Advice Bureaux and county courts

(under 'Courts' in the telephone directory), explains in some detail how to sue and defend actions without a solicitor. Below is a brief summary of the procedure.

* Write to the trader explaining that if he does not resolve your complaint within seven days, you will issue court proceedings against him.

* Decide whom you are going to sue and make sure you get the name and address right. When you sue a limited company (one which has Ltd, Limited, or PLC after its name on its headed notepaper) the summons must be served at its registered office. The address should be on its notepaper and bills or you can write to or telephone the Registrar of Companies. If the business is not a limited company, you should send the summons to its business address and to the homes of its partners. You will want to sue both the business and the individuals involved in order to stand the best chance of getting redress. The law says that any business which operates under a name other than that of its owner must display the name and address of the owner or owners on its business premises and on its stationery.

* Decide where you are going to sue.
  * If you are suing a limited company you can use the court for the district where the registered office is located.
  * If you are suing an unlimited company you can use the court for the district where the business you are suing is located or where its partners live.
  * Alternatively you can opt for the court for the district where the *cause of action* – the events that led to the case – occurred. As this will often be your local court, you will probably choose this option.

The person you are suing (the defendant) can apply to have the case transferred and it is up to the court to decide where it should be heard.

Alec Smart ordered some curtains costing £150 from a salesman who called at his home. When they arrived they were a completely different fabric from the one he had chosen from the salesman's sample. He wrote to the company rejecting them as he was entitled to do under the Sale of Goods Act because they were not 'as described' and claiming his money back. The company ignored his letters, so Alec decided to sue them using the small claims procedure in the county court. The company's registered office was 75 miles away but, because Alec had signed the contract in his own home, this was where the 'cause of action' occurred. So Alec was able to sue in his local county court.

* Next, prepare your **particulars of claim,** which will be attached to the summons. You can do this either on your own plain paper or on a form available from the court. Put the name of the court at the top with a space for the case number, which will be allocated later. Then give the names and addresses of the defendant (the person or business you are suing) and the plaintiff (yourself). Below that, set out in numbered paragraphs:

- the facts that have led up to the case, such as where and when you bought the goods or services, who from, what they cost and what was wrong with them. Keep the information brief – you are not so much stating your case as letting the court and the defendant know what the claim is about.
- the amount you are claiming and how this sum is broken down. If your new washing machine flooded the kitchen, ruining the lino, you might claim the price of the washing machine and the cost of replacing the flooring.
- whether you would like the case to be dealt with under the small claims procedure, if the defendant disputes your claim.

When you are preparing these particulars refer to yourself as 'the plantiff' and the trader as 'the defendant' rather than using 'I' and 'he'. Write clearly or type, and make a copy for yourself, one for each defendant and one for the court.

* Go to your nearest county court and fill out a **request** form to issue a summons. Send or take this to the Chief Clerk at the court where you are suing, together with the fees for issuing and serving the summons, a copy of the particulars of claim for the court and one for each of the defendants and a self-addressed envelope. The court fee depends on the amount you are claiming: at present fees range from £7 to £37. You will be asked whether you want a **default summons** or a **fixed date summons.** If you are claiming only money, you will want the first. If not, you want the second.

* When the court has prepared a summons, you will be sent a **plaint** (case) **note** which includes the number allocated to your case. Keep this carefully and quote the number in any dealings with the court.

* If a *default summons* has been issued, no hearing date is fixed. Once he receives the summons, the defendant has 14 days in which to act. He can:

  ● pay your claim in full.
  ● admit your claim but ask for time to pay. You must decide within 14 days whether or not to accept his proposals. If you reject them, both you and the defendant will be asked to meet the registrar to work out a way of paying the money owed. If you cannot attend this appointment, tell the court.
  ● offer to settle out of court. He will probably offer less than the full amount you are claiming and you will have to decide whether or not to accept. Seek advice if you are unsure. When you write to the defendant about a compromise, head your letters 'without prejudice' so that he cannot use them in court if the matter does go to trial or arbitration. If you accept an out-of-court settlement, make sure the defendant has paid the money into court before you let the court know you are pulling out.

- do nothing. At the end of 14 days you can apply to the court to have judgment entered against the defendant. This can be done by post, if you supply a stamped addressed envelope. However, if you are claiming damages which have to be decided by the court, you should apply for an appointment with the registrar.
- lodge a defence and/or put in a counterclaim against you. If he does this, you will be sent a copy. The court will then notify you that it has arranged a pre-trial review or fixed a date for the arbitration itself.

If a *fixed date summons* has been issued, you will be given a date for the pre-trial review or the arbitration. Let the court know if this is not convenient.

---

* The pre-trial review (which is not held in all cases and courts) is an informal private meeting between the registrar and both parties to see if the matter can be settled and, if not, to discuss what will happen next. The registrar may ask you or the defendant to provide more information and each party can ask the other about anything not clear about the case. You are both entitled to know what facts the other party has based his case upon and you must disclose all the documents you have that are relevant to the case. You should therefore bring these along to the pre-trial review. If the matter is not settled at this stage – and it may well be - a date for the arbitration hearing will be fixed. Tell the registrar if there are any dates when you or your witnesses cannot attend.

If the defendant does not show up at the pre-trial review, you may be able to get judgment against him. You will have to prove your case to the registrar – another reason why you should take all your documents along.

---

* It is up to the registrar to decide how an arbitration hearing is conducted. You can usually take a friend or relative along to 'hold your hand', take notes and give you whispered advice, though some registrars may object to this. If you have consulted a consumer adviser

he may be prepared to come with you but will not be able to present the case – only you, a solicitor or barrister can do that. If you have not employed a solicitor and find that the other side has, do not immediately despair. If you present your case well and have a sympathetic registrar, you should not be at a disadvantage.

The way you present your case is important. As the registrar author of the booklet *Small Claims in the County Court* points out, 'a party who appears calm and reasonable creates a better impression than one who is filled with indignation.' **Assume that the registrar knows nothing about your case and describe the train of events, slowly, calmly and without exaggerating.**

After you have put your case, the registrar will probably ask you some questions. He may then ask to hear from your witnesses or he may call the defendant. The defendant will have a chance to question you and your witnesses and you to question him and his witnesses. The registrar will usually deliver his judgment on the spot, once he has listened to all the evidence. He may reserve judgment, in which case you will be sent a notice telling you when to attend court for the judgment.

---

*   If you win, you can ask the court to order the defendant to pay your court fees, and witnesses' expenses. You can also claim any necessary expenses you have incurred, such as the cost of photocopying, fares or an overnight stay in a hotel to attend the hearing. Time off work for you and your witnesses may also be allowed, but this is unusual in arbitration. If you lose, the defendant can ask the court to order *you* to pay these costs. It is up to the registrar to decide what costs to allow.

---

*   If you win, the defendant will be ordered to pay whatever the registrar decides is owed to you. The defendant may pay up at once or he may ask to pay by instalments. If he wants to pay by instalments and the court agrees, you can either accept or reject his proposals. If you reject them you will have a chance to question him about his means at a special examination. The registrar will then decide how the money should be paid.

Unfortunately, not all defendants pay up graciously. Some cannot pay, others choose not to. It is up to you – not the court – to take steps to recover your money. This can be time-consuming, tedious, expensive and un-rewarding (see below, pages 265–6). A small, but significant, proportion of consumers who win their case receive no money at all or only part of what they are lawfully owed.

Preparing your case
You may think that the facts of your case as you know them speak for themselves and that only a fool would disagree with your assessment. The defendant may feel the same way, so it is essential to get as much sound evidence together as you can to back up your claim. This may take the form of:

* documents, such as a contract, invoices, receipts and correspondence
* your own version of events
* statements from witnesses

As I have remarked in previous chapters, it is always a good idea to keep the paperwork relating to trans-actions you make – whether it is an invoice for a car repair, a contract for a new kitchen, or the brochure description of a package holiday. This documentation can provide vital evidence if you find yourself in court.

Keeping a diary of events can also be useful. Once a problem arises with something you have ordered or bought, start recording brief details of all the efforts you make to sort the matter out. Make short notes, with dates, of any conversations you have with the trader either by phone or in person, recording what was said and to whom you spoke. Keep copies of all correspon-dence. This can be a helpful *aide memoire* when you are preparing your own evidence.

Written statements from witnesses are sometimes allowed when a case is brought under the small claims procedure. So statements from other holidaymakers at your abysmal Mediterranean hotel to the effect that they all had food poisoning and found bugs in the bed could be useful. But the registrar may decide that such statements are worthless – as you could have forged the lot – and may not accept them.

If the money at stake justifies the cost, you could consider asking a witness who is an expert in the relevant field to prepare a report. If the other party agrees, this report can be shown to the registrar at the hearing. Otherwise, you will have to call the expert to court, which can work out expensive because, if you lose, you will have to foot the bill. In certain types of case, the evidence of an expert witness can be crucial.

Alec Smart bought a year-old saloon from D. Fraud, car dealers. He was assured that it was 'a beautiful runner', which had belonged to a teacher who had decided to trade up-market when he was promoted. Things started to go wrong almost immediately, but Mr Fraud never seemed to be available when Alec called. So Alec had the car repaired at another garage. They told him they'd seen it before – when it had been involved in a crash, written off by the owner's insurers and sold for scrap. An engineer from one of the motoring organisations confirmed that the chassis had indeed been reconstructed. Alec took the first garage to court, presented the engineer's report and had judgment entered against D. Fraud, who did not defend the case.

Finding an expert witness is not always easy. Who do you turn to when your leather coat is ruined by the dry cleaners and the culprit alleges that there was a fault in the skin, or your carpet goes bald after a year and the shop claims that you have spilled acid on it? When you are looking for expert witnesses try:

* a Citizens' Advice Bureau or Consumer Advice Centre
* the trading standards or consumer protection department at your local council offices

* a trade association or professional body
* a local technical college
* a well-established and respected local firm.

When the loser won't pay up
As I have already pointed out, it is your responsibility – not the court's – to make sure you get any money owed to you. A losing defendant should pay the money to you or to the court, which will pass it on to you. But the court will not let you know if the debtor has defaulted.

If you don't receive your money, contact the court to find out what is happening. If the defendant has defaulted, you will have to make an application to court to have the judgment enforced. This takes time and costs money – though you can claim enforcement costs back from the defendant if you eventually nail him – so once again you should make sure that the defendant can afford to pay. You can compel him to come to court and answer questions about his resources: by asking the right questions about his finances you will be able to decide what method to use to recover your money. Refusing to answer these questions is contempt of court. Some defendants will pay up at this stage rather than attend court or risk breaking the law. If yours does come to court, ask him how much he has in his wallet: he may have enough to settle your claim on the spot!

If you do have to enforce judgment, seek the help of the court officials. And have patience. The main ways of enforcing a money judgment in the county court are:

● **a warrant of execution.** You pay a fee and instruct a court bailiff to seize the debtor's goods and auction them to pay the debt. This is the most often-used method of enforcement. It usually takes several weeks and may not be successful.

● **attachment of earnings.** You pay a fee and apply to the court for the debtor's employer to deduct money from his wage packet to meet your debt over a period of time. You cannot use this method if the debtor is self-employed.

- **garnishee proceedings.** You pay a fee and apply to the court for money in the debtor's bank account to be frozen and used to pay your debt. You must know exactly where the account is and whose name it is in.

These methods of enforcement are fairly simple and you can organise them yourself with the help of court officials. There are other remedies, but they are more complicated, more appropriate for larger debts and should not be undertaken without the help of a solicitor. They include:

- **a charging order.** You apply to the court for a 'charge' on one of the debtor's assets – usually his house. You must know the exact address of the property. When the house is sold, the money owed to you will come out of the proceeds.

- **appointment of a receiver.** If the debtor owns a property or a business from which he obtains an income, you can apply to court for a receiver to be appointed to collect the income to pay the money owed to you.

Larger claims

If you are claiming more than £500, the matter will not normally be dealt with under the small claims procedure. You can apply for arbitration in disputes involving more than £500 if the defendant agrees: it will be up to the registrar to decide whether this is appropriate.

The steps for taking a case to trial in the county court outside the small claims procedure are similar to those described above, but the rules for the preparation of the case and the hearing itself are much stricter and less flexible. The other fundamental difference is that both sides are usually represented by solicitors or barristers. You can conduct your own case if you wish, but you should remember:

* Court proceedings can be rather intimidating if you are unfamiliar with them. The rules with which you have

to comply can seem very technical and difficult to understand.

* The other party may well be legally represented so you could be at a disadvantage.
* The losing party normally pays the other side's solicitor's costs, which may be considerable.

Do not dismiss legal action out of hand just because your claim is above the limit for the small claims procedure. Many firms of solicitors will give you a half-hour preliminary interview for £5, so it is always worth seeking advice on whether you have a case and whether you are likely to qualify for legal aid. (See Chapter 6 for more on using a solicitor.)

Addresses of Organisations Mentioned in this Book

Action for the Victims of Medical
  Accidents
24 Southwark Street
London SE1 1TY
01 403 4744

Advertising Standards Authority
Brook House
Torrington Place
London WC1E 7HN
01 580 5555

Advisory Committee on
  Telecommunications
For England:
Atlantic House
Holborn Viaduct
London EC1N 2HQ
01 353 4020

For Wales:
Caradog House (1st Floor)
St Andrews Place
Cardiff CF1 3PW
0222 374028

For Scotland:
Alhambra House
45 Waterloo Street
Glasgow G2 6AT
041 248 2855, ext 253

For Northern Ireland:
Chamber of Commerce and
  Industry
22 Great Victoria Street
Belfast BT2 7PU
0232 244113

Air Transport Users' Committee
129 Kingsway
London WC2B 6NN
01 242 3882

Approved Coal Merchants'
  Scheme
Victoria House
Southampton Row
London WC1B 4DH
01 405 1601

Architects' Registration Council
  of the United Kingdom
73 Hallam Street
London W1N 6EE
01 580 5861

Association of British Insurers
Aldermary House
Queen Street
London EC4N 1TT
01 248 4477

Association of British Travel
  Agents
55–57 Newman Street
London W1P 4AH
01 637 2444

Association of British Laundry,
  Cleaning and Rental Services
Lancaster Gate House
319 Pinner Road
Harrow
Middlesex HA1 3HX
01 863 7755

Association of British Credit
  Unions
Credit Union Centre
PO Box 135
High Street
Skelmersdale
Lancashire WN8 8AP
0695 32423

Association of Community
  Health Councils
c/o Nurses Home
Langton Place
Wren Street
London WC1X 0HD
01 833 4456

Association of Manufacturers of
  Domestic Electrical Appliances
Leicester House
4 Leicester Street
London WC2H 7BN
01 437 0678

Association of Optical
  Practitioners
233–234 Blackfriars Road
London SE1 8NW
01 261 9661

Association of Photographic
  Laboratories
9 Warwick Court
Gray's Inn
London WC1R 5DJ
01 405 2762/4253

Automobile Association (AA)
Fanum House
Basingstoke
Hampshire RG21 2EA
0256 20123

Banking Ombudsman
Citadel House
5–11 Fetter Lane
London EC4A 1BR
01 583 1395

Bar Council
11 South Square
Gray's Inn
London WC1R 5EL
01 242 0082

British Association of Removers
279 Gray's Inn Road
London WC1X 8SY
01 837 3088

British Dental Association
64 Wimpole Street
London W1M 8AL
01 935 0875

British Direct Marketing
  Association
1 New Oxford Street
London WC1A 1NQ
01 242 2254

British Electrotechnical
   Approvals Board
Mark House
9–11 Queen's Road
Hersham
Walton-on-Thames
Surrey KT12 5NA
09322 44401

British Gas Corporation
Rivermill House
152 Grosvenor Road
London SW1V 3JL
01 821 1444

British Hotels, Restaurants and
   Caterers Association
40 Duke Street
London W1M 6HR
01 499 6641

British Insurance Brokers'
   Association
BIBA House
14 Bevis Marks
London EC3A 7NT
01 623 9043

British Institute of Professional
   Photography
Amwell End
Ware
Hertfordshire SG12 9HN
0920 4011

British Photographic Association
7–15 Lansdowne Road
Croydon
Surrey CR9 2PL
01 688 4422

British Photographic Importers'
   Association
7–15 Lansdowne Road
Croydon
Surrey CR9 2PL
01 688 4422

British Standards Institution
2 Park Street
London W1A 2BS
01 629 9000

British Telecom
British Telecom Centre
81 Newgate Street
London EC1A 7AJ
01 356 5000

Building Employers'
   Confederation
82 New Cavendish Street
London W1M 8AD
01 580 5588

Details of Guarantee Scheme
   from:
BEC Building Trust Ltd
Invicta House
London Road
Maidstone
Kent ME16 8JH
0622 683791

Building Societies Association
3 Savile Row
London W1X 1AF
01 437 0655

Central Services Agency
25 Adelaide Street
Belfast BT2 8FD
0232 224431

Civil Aviation Authority
CAA House
45 Kingsway
London WC2B 6TE
01 379 7311

Chartered Association of
   Certified Accountants
29 Lincoln's Inn Fields
London WC2A 3EE
01 242 6855

Chartered Institute of Arbitrators
75 Cannon Street
London EC4N 5BH
01 236 8761

Confederation for the
  Registration of Gas Installers
  (CORGI)
St Martin's House
140 Tottenham Court Road
London W1P 9LN
01 387 9185

Consumer Credit Public Register
Office of Fair Trading
Government Building
Bromyard Avenue
London W3 7BB
01 743 5566

Consumers' Association
14 Buckingham Street
London WC2N 6DS
01 839 1222

Council of Licensed
  Conveyancers
Golden Cross House
Duncannon Street
London WC2N 4JF
01 210 4602

Department of Economic
  Development (Trading
  Standards Branch)
176 Newtownbreda Road
Belfast BT8 4QS
0232 647151

Department of Energy
Thames House South
Millbank
London SW1P 4QJ
01 211 3000

Department of the Environment
2 Marsham Street
London SW1P 3EB
01 212 3434

Department of Environment for
  Northern Ireland
Parliament Building
Stormont
Belfast BT4 3SY
0232 63210

Department of Health and Social
  Security
Alexander Fleming House
Elephant and Castle
London SE1 6BY
01 407 5522

Department of Trade and
  Industry
1 Victoria Street
London SW1H 0ET
01 215 7877

Insurance Division
Sanctuary Buildings
16–20 Great Smith Street
London SW1P 3DB
01 215 7877

Design Centre
28 Haymarket
London SW1Y 4SU
01 839 8000

Direct Selling Association
44 Russell Square
London WC1B 4JP
01 580 8433

Domestic Coal Consumers'
  Council
Gavrelle House
2 Bunhill Row
Freepost
London EC1B 1DT
01 638 8914/8929

Electrical Contractors'
  Association
ESCA House
34 Palace Court
London W2 4HY
01 229 1266

Electricity Consumers' Council
Brook House
2–16 Torrington Place
London WC1E 7LL
01 636 5703

Electricity Council
30 Millbank
London SW1T 4RD
01 834 2333

Federation of Master Builders
Gordon Fisher House
33 John Street
London WC1N 3BB
01 242 7583

Financial Intermediaries,
  Managers and Brokers
  Regulatory Association
  (FIMBRA)
22 Great Tower Street
London EC3R 5AQ
01 283 4814

Footwear Distributors'
  Federation
Commonwealth House
1–19 New Oxford Street
London WC1A 1PA
01 404 0955

Gas Consumers' Council
162 Regent Street
London W1R 5TB
01 439 0012

General Consumer Council for
  Northern Ireland
Elizabeth House
116 Holywood Road
Belfast BT4 1NY
0232 672 488

General Dental Council
37 Wimpole Street
London W1M 8DQ
01 486 2171

General Medical Council
44 Hallam Street
London W1N 6AE
01 580 7642

General Optical Council
41 Harley Street
London W1N 2DJ
01 580 3898

Glass and Glazing Federation
44–48 Borough High Street
London SE1 1XB
01 403 7177

Good Housekeeping Institute
National Magazine House
72 Broadwick Street
London W1V 2BP
01 439 7144

Guaranteed Treatments
  Protection Trust
PO Box 77
27 London Road
High Wycombe
Buckinghamshire HP11 1BW
0494 447049

Health Service Commissioner
For England and Northern
  Ireland:
Church House
Great Smith Street
London SW1P 3BW
01 212 7676

For Wales:
Pearl Assurance House
Greyfriars Road
Cardiff CF1 3AG
0222 394621

For Scotland:
11 Melville Crescent
Edinburgh EH3 7LU
031 225 7465

Heating and Ventilating
  Contractors' Association
ESCA House
34 Palace Court
London W2 4JG
01 229 2488

Incorporated Association of
  Architects and Surveyors
Jubilee House
Billing Brook Road
Weston Favell
Northampton NN3 4NW
0604 404121

Incorporated Society of Valuers
  and Auctioneers
3 Cadogan Gate
London SW1X 0AS
01 235 2282

Independent Broadcasting
  Authority
70 Brompton Road
London SW3 1EY
01 584 7011

Independent Footwear Retailers'
  Association
109 Headstone Road
Harrow
Middlesex HA1 1PG
01 427 1545

Institute for Complementary
  Medicine
21 Portland Place
London W1N 3AF
01 636 9543

Institute of Chartered
  Accountants in England and
  Wales
PO Box 433
Chartered Accountants' Hall
Moorgate Place
London EC2P 2BJ
01 628 7060

Institute of Chartered
  Accountants in Scotland
27 Queen Street
Edinburgh EH2 1LA
031 225 5673

Institute of Chartered
  Accountants in Ireland
(Northern Ireland branch)
11 Donegal Square South
Belfast BT1 5JE
0232 221600

Institute of Plumbing
64 Station Lane
Hornchurch
Essex RM12 6NB
04024 72791

Insurance Brokers' Registration
  Council
15 St Helen's Place
London EC3A 6DS
01 588 4387

Insurance Ombudsman Bureau
31 Southampton Row
London WC1B 5HJ
01 242 8613

Law Centres Federation
Duchess House
18–19 Warren Street
London W1P 5DB
01 387 8570

Law Society
For England and Wales:
113 Chancery Lane
London WC2A 1PL
01 242 1222

For Scotland:
26–27 Drumsheugh Gardens
Edinburgh EH3 7YR
031 226 7411

For Northern Ireland:
Royal Courts of Justice
Chichester Street
Belfast BT1 3JZ
0232 231614

Lay Observer
For England and Wales:
Royal Courts of Justice
Strand
London WC2A 2LL
01 405 7641

For Scotland:
22 Melville Street
Edinburgh EH3 7NS
031 225 3236

For Northern Ireland:
IDB House
64 Chichester Street
Belfast BT1 4LE
0232 233233

Lord Chancellor's Department
Neville House
Page Street
London SW1P 4LS
01 211 3000

Lloyd's
London House
London Street
London EC3R 7AB
01 623 7100

Mailing Preference Service
Freepost 22
London W1E 7EZ
01 378 7244

Mail Order Publishers'
  Authority
1 New Burlington Street
London W1X 1FD
01 437 0706

Mail Order Traders' Association
25 Castle Street
Liverpool L2 4TD
051 236 7581

Master Photographers'
  Association
1 West Ruislip Station
West Ruislip
Middlesex HA4 7DW
08956 30876

Ministry of Agriculture, Fisheries
  and Food
Whitehall Place
London SW1A 2HH
01 233 3000

Motor Agents' Association
201 Great Portland Street
London W1N 6AB
01 580 9122

National Conciliation Service
73 Park Street
Bristol BS1 5PS
0272 293232

Motor Cycle Association
Starley House
Eaton Road
Coventry CV1 2FH

Motorcycle Retailers' Association
31a High Street
Tunbridge Wells
Kent TN1 1XN
0892 26081

Multiple Shoe Retailers'
  Association
Commonwealth House
1–19 New Oxford Street
London WC1A 1PA
01 404 0955

National Association of Citizens'
  Advice Bureaux
Myddleton House
115–123 Pentonville Road
London N1 9LZ
01 833 2181

National Association of Estate
  Agents
Arbon House
21 Jury Street
Warwick CV34 4EH
0926 496800

National Association of Funeral
  Directors
57 Doughty Street
London WC1N 2NE
01 242 9388

National Association of Multiple
  Shoe Repairers
60 Wickham Hill
Hurstpierpoint
Hassocks
Sussex BN6 9NP
07918 3488

National Association of Retail
  Furnishers
17–21 George Street
Croydon CR9 1TQ
01 680 8444

National Cavity Insulation
  Association
PO Box 12
Haslemere
Surrey GU27 3AN
0428 54011

National Consumer Council
20 Grosvenor Gardens
London SW1W 0DH
01 730 3469

National Federation of Consumer
  Groups
12 Mosley Street
Newcastle upon Tyne NE1 1DE
0632 618259

National House Building Council
  (NHBC)
53 Portland Place
London W1N 4BU
01 637 1248

National Inspection Council for
  Electrical Installation
  Contracting (NICEIC)
Vintage House
36–37 Albert Embankment
London SE1 7UJ
01 582 7746

National Pharmaceutical
  Association
Mallinson House
40–42 St Peter's Street
St Albans
Hertfordshire AL1 3NP
0727 32161

Northern Ireland Coal Advisory
　Service
87 Eglantine Avenue
Belfast BT9 6EW
0232 681331

Office of Fair Trading
Field House
Breams Buildings
London EC4A 1PR
01 242 2858

Office of Telecommunications
　(OFTEL)
Atlantic House
Holborn Viaduct
London EC1N 2HQ
01 353 4020

Patients' Association
Room 33
18 Charing Cross Road
London WC2H 0HR
01 240 0671

Personal Insurance Arbitration
　Service (PIAS)
Chartered Institute of Arbitrators
75 Cannon Street
London EC4N 5BH
01 236 8761

Pharmaceutical Society of Great
　Britain
1 Lambeth High Street
London SE1 7JN
01 735 9141

Post Office Headquarters
33 Grosvenor Place
London SW1X 1PX
01 235 8000

Post Office Users' National
　Council
Waterloo Bridge House
Waterloo Road
London SE1 8UA
01 928 9458

Post Office Users' Council for
　Wales
2 Park Grove
Cardiff CF1 3BN
0222 374028

Post Office Users' Council for
　Scotland
Alhambra House
45 Waterloo Street
Glasgow G2 6AT
041 248 2855

Post Office Users' Council for
　Northern Ireland
Chamber of Commerce
22 Great Victoria Street
Belfast BT2 7PU
0232 244113

Radio, Electrical and Television
　Retailers' Association
57–61 Newington Causeway
London SE1 6BE
01 403 1463

Registrar of Companies
For England and Wales:
Companies House
Crown Way
Maindy
Cardiff CF4 3UZ
0222 388588

For Scotland:
102 George Street
Edinburgh EH2 3DJ
031 225 5774

For Northern Ireland:
43–47 Chichester Street
Belfast BT1 4RJ
0232 234121

Royal Automobile Club (RAC)
49 Pall Mall
London SW1Y 5JG
01 839 7050

Royal Incorporation of Architects
in Scotland
15 Rutland Square
Edinburgh EH1 2BE
031 229 7205

Royal Institute of British
Architects
66 Portland Place
London W1N 4AD
01 580 5533

Royal Institution of Chartered
Surveyors
12 Great George Street
Parliament Square
London SW1P 3AD
01 222 7000

Royal Society of Ulster Architects
2 Mount Charles
Belfast BT7 1NZ
0232 223760

Scottish Consumer Council
314 St Vincent Street
Glasgow G3 8XW
041 226 5261

Scottish Development
Department (Housing Branch)
St Andrew's House
Regent Road
Edinburgh EH1 3DE
031 556 8501

Scottish House Furnishers'
Association
203 Pitt Street
Glasgow G2 4DB
041 332 6381

Scottish Motor Trade Association
3 Palmerston Place
Edinburgh EH12 5AQ
031 225 3643

SHAC (London Housing Aid
Centre)
189a Old Brompton Road
London SW5 0AR
01 373 7276

Shelter
157 Waterloo Road
London SE1 8XF
01 633 9377

Society of Master Shoe Repairers
St Crispin's House
Station Road
Desborough
Northants
0536 760374

Society of Motor Manufacturers
and Traders
Forbes House
Halkin Street
London SW1X 7DS
01 235 7000

Society of Motor Auctions
Pilkington House
Richmond Road
Trafford Park
Manchester M17 1RE
0532 536540

Solicitors' Complaints Bureau
Portland House
Stag Place
London SW1E 5BL
01 834 2288

d Fuel Advisory Service
bart House
rosvenor Place
London SW1X 7AE
01 235 2020

Vehicle Builders' and Repairers'
  Association
Belmont House
102 Finkle Lane
Gildersome
Leeds LS27 7TW
0532 538333

Water Authorities Association
1 Queen Anne's Gate
London
SW1H 9BT
01 222 8111

Welsh Consumer Council
Castle Buildings
Womanby Street
Cardiff
CF1 2BN
0222 396056

Index